THE OFFERING

Night is Falling

For Your sake we are being killed all the day long;
we are regarded as sheep to be slaughtered.
Romans 8:36

A meditation on Prophetic Scripture
and its message for Our Time

by
Dr. Marc Erickson

Author's Note:

The thesis of this book is that the end of this present evil world is important to God. He created our world to be a place of discovery and of opportunity to choose God after experiencing Him. God loves the world and will redeem an inordinately large number of sinners in the days leading to the End. The preponderance of prophetic Scripture is given to prepare God's people to be his 'Angel of the Lord' by their living and by their dying. This work presents an attempt to harmonize three sources of truth in clarifying what is happening as the Lord returns to gather His people to Himself.

TABLE OF CONTENTS

THREE: THE BIBLE, GOD'S WORD   55

PROPHETIC WORDS

REVELATION LIGHT 1-20

JESUS TO HIS ANGEL TO JOHN

PREFACE

*I*n August of 2015, my wife and I, together with a small team from our church, were invited to help staff a new school in the West Bank, located in the village of Beit Sahour. Beit Sahour is part of what used to be called the Christian Triangle. We found the people there to be the kindest, most humble, hard-working families we have ever lived among. Christians are still the majority in Beit Sahour, but each year they are under increasing pressure to leave, both from Israel and their Muslim neighbors. Many have emigrated to safer lands, but others stay on saying, "We must not sell out and move. We are Palestinians. We have suffered persecution as Christians here for centuries and survived. Our families live well here, and we want our children to grow up knowing their grandparents and many cousins." It has been very special to talk with them and to hear both their hopes and fears. ISIS, a murderous movement (or *Daesh* as it is called locally), is raging just over the border. Recently we heard new reports of mass graves being uncovered in Palmyra, Syria, filled with Christians who refused to renounce Christ. Parents and little children stood together and died for their faith.

There have also been mass killings in Turkey and northern Iraq among the Assyrian and Armenian churches during the last century. Today the Syrian and Chaldean churches are on the run. Life for the Palestinians under Israeli occupation has been full of humiliations, and because of this, two uprisings, called *intifadas*, have occurred. The believers in Christ from every denomination and communion now number less than one percent of the West Bank population. Fifty years ago their numbers were closer to thirty percent.

As I listen to Christian pastors, businesspeople, priests, laymen, and educators, all highly intelligent and excelling in their chosen professions, I hear agreement among them on one startling conviction. The only hope Israel or Palestine or Muslims or atheists or secular hedonists have in this area is Jesus Christ. Christians, therefore, need to become Kingdom people who can see past politics, ethnic strife and looming worldwide evil, and become the Body of Christ for all their friends and enemies to see. These people of conviction are growing in number. We met them in Egypt, Jordan, Lebanon, Syria, and Turkey. They speak wisely about the power of prayer, the credibility that comes when they love, honor and serve each other, and the need for the Church at large to join them in denying self, taking up their cross daily until we die for truth or Jesus comes for us.

A dear friend listened as I recounted a recent report,

I'd heard of four men hung for their faith in a neighboring country and he added these details. When they put the noose around the fourth man's neck, they told him, "We will release you if you willingly renounce Jesus and return to Islam." The man spoke out, "How can I renounce Christ? I see Him coming for me right now."

This book is about the calling of the Church to preach the Gospel of the Kingdom as a testimony to the nations all the way through to the End. Many of our Palestinian brothers and sisters are doing that now as **the Night is falling on their land.**

The burden of this book is also addressed in a vision experienced by a precious Christian friend while a student in Rome. With her permission I am sharing it as preparation to look seriously at the Lord's promise of persecution that is about to engulf the Church worldwide as the end of this Age draws near.

Experienced on February 16, 1999

I was attending Mass at St. Peter's Basilica at the front-most altar of the Chair of Peter with its beautiful alabaster Holy Spirit window. At the consecration, the priest's voice seemed to have a certain urgency in it which chilled me. Suddenly I clearly saw, and entered myself, into a vision of that same place entirely in ruins. The actual edifice of St. Peter's grand basilica was destroyed. Mass was being held in the rubble on the same spot, and white smoke was rising from the piles of rubble. It was daytime, and the bluish white sky opened above the scene where the towering roof of the Basilica had once been. The destruction was complete. You wouldn't have known it was a church but for the position of the people.

The Mass was at the distribution of communion. There was one priest vested (in red and gold?) and the people were going up in a single file line and then walking away to the left and the right - as if to return to their seats. However, it was understood in the vision that each person would be killed as they walked away having received communion. We all knew it in the scene, but it deterred no one. The stream of communicants was steady, and an atmosphere of peace, total peace, prevailed. Who or what was on the periphery was not visible - but it was this presence enforcing the understood persecution.

I intended to take communion. It was also understood that the priest would be killed when he finished distributing communion. The overwhelming thing to me was the peace of each individual, as well as the way in which no one was deterred by fear from being there and going up to receive communion.

That is all - then the vision ended, and it was the actual Mass again, within the walls of the beautiful Basilica, and I went up with everyone else to receive communion - but this powerful vision has stayed with my heart ever since. At the time I felt that this vision was symbolic of future persecution which the Church might undergo. I now feel I was seeing the aftermath of an actual attack on the Basilica. The physical attack and the post-communion persecution may be separate events.[1]

Note how this simple account illustrates the Angel's words to Daniel in Scripture, while adding the promise of God's peace abiding in and empowering the martyrs of the last days:

The man clothed in linen, who was above the waters of the river, lifted his right hand and his left hand toward heaven,

---

[1] A vision experienced by Elizabeth A. Mitchell, Ph.D., Wisconsin, USA, while a Doctoral student in Rome

and I heard him swear by him who lives forever, saying, "It will be for a time, times and half a time. When the power of the holy people has been finally broken, all these things will be completed. (Da 12:7)

A War is in progress between God's People of Truth and the Arch Liar, the Devil. The gift of a book on philosophy in 1960, *Philosophy and the Christian Faith*, by Colin Brown, revealed to me the power of presuppositions and world views to shape human behavior.

An additional text given me by a young missionary surgeon in 1967, *Escape from Reason*, by Francis Schaeffer, forced me to look at the conflict being played out between contemporary philosophies and Christianity. Schaeffer turned a crisis of faith in his own life into a ministry seeking to help other young intellectuals at a retreat center in Switzerland called L'Abri. In his writings I discovered that the existence of authentic truth depended on knowing and interacting with God. The catastrophe of losing truth comes when one allows modernity to swallow up our Christian transcendent revelation. And of course who hasn't been lifted up and educated by C.S. Lewis in his works including *Mere Christianity, The Problem of Pain, The Space Trilogy,* and *The Narnia Series.*

In 2015, I celebrated my 75th birthday. A lot has happened in the world during this short period of time. In 1945 the world entered the nuclear Age and the possibility of man ending all life on this planet became a realistic possibility. Atomic bombs gave way to Hydrogen bombs which gave way to Neutron bombs that would kill people and spare buildings. The advances in weapons of mass destruction accelerated to nerve gas and biologic toxins (like weaponized anthrax and smallpox virus). The doctrine of mutual assured destruction for only a brief time became a defining moderating factor constraining superpower politics. This mutual restraint maintained a semblance of stability until recently, when people have come on the world scene, namely Islamic extremists, of whom some see catastrophic destruction as the only way to transform the world.

Sometime in the early 1980's the notion of linking up the computers of the earth by a world wide web became a reality. Suddenly via clever search engines the people of earth gained access to vast amounts of data and instant knowledge about events taking place around the world. This launched the building of a new undivided global culture. The internet, supported by satellites, has since potentially connected every human being with every human being. The barriers of language and geography imposed at Babel have been substantially overcome.

The 1990's saw the rise of an ideology that quickly became resident in the universities: Post Modernism and the notion that truth doesn't exist. The structures of truth, therefore, needed to be deconstructed. So countless college freshman for the past 30 years have been returning home to the parents who were paying dearly for their education with a deconstructionist view of every precious conviction of the meaning of life these parents held. The ensuing decades have revealed how easy it was to relegate deep religious convictions and political history to the ash heap and leave only emotions and human relational needs to fill the void of what life should be.

In the last seven years, in reaction to several ill-conceived foreign initiatives by the Western Democracies, the leadership of the last remaining superpower, the United States of America, with the support of its electorate, began the process of voluntarily abrogating much of its leadership responsibilities in the world. The decision was made to support a United Nations Consortium with no real power to accomplish anything in the way of restraining lawlessness, the heinous killing of innocent people, or the self-serving economic policies that impoverish smaller nations. Into this failure of political nerve has come the rise of many nuclear armed competing hegemonies that are hardening into a new world of disorder, including Shia Iran, Russia, China, India, Pakistan, France, Britain, the Unites States, Israel, and North Korea.

Absent any working theory of the future, the world is anxious and ill-prepared to restrain the rise of radically evil visionaries and ego-driven nationalists who see the present situation as an opportunity to implement their destructive visions. All serious thinkers must ask this question daily as we go forward in time: when will the wars stop and peace take hold instead?

Shortly after VE day[2] I remember as a five-year-old standing by my Mother as she was washing dishes, asking her a question that was burning in my heart. "Mother, now that the *Nazis* have been defeated, is there a new enemy of our country that we must fight?"

Without hesitation this dear woman, whose husband had just spent several years in the US Chaplaincy Corps during the War, looked back at me and said sadly, "Well,

---

[2] Victory in Europe, WW2

there are the Russians."

I was disturbed by her answer and felt anxious that we were not finished with War. A few years later I learned as I was eavesdropping on my father and some of his pastoral friends that SAC (the Strategic Air Command) had just announced that it would from now on have at least half of its planes in the air to protect us against surprise attack from the USSR. That is how the Cold War entered the thinking of a seven-year-old boy. Soon after, Mao Zedong stood before a million people in Tiananmen Square and announced, "The East is Red." The Korean 'Police Action" followed along with Hydrogen Bomb tests and dangerous radioactive fallout. The entire world sobered up. When the Reverend Billy Graham went on the radio weekly, saying "This is the Hour of Decision", we all knew he was right.

Today more than 2.3 Billion people across the globe give some kind of allegiance to Jesus Christ. During the past century more people have died for their commitment to Christ than in all of the previous 1900 years combined. The seven-year-old in his mother's kitchen is now 75 years old, and the same question fills his thinking. Now that the Cold War between two superpowers is ended and only one superpower remains, are we finished with War? The Prophet Daniel 2500 years ago, looking beyond the predicted destruction of the second Temple and the city of Jerusalem, heard the angel Gabriel say, "The end will come like a flood: War will continue until the end, and desolations have been decreed."[3]

This book will attempt to give answers to what the two great Divine Revelations have to say about our present

---

[3] Dn 9:26

reality and the looming evidence that the End of the world as we know it is imminent. Three sources will be accessed in this study. The First Source, the Book of Nature, will be examined as compiled and organized by the Ongoing Scientific Enterprise. It is the conviction of the author that the Book of Nature, rightly read, is becoming more and more congruent with the Second Source, the Book of Human History, and its center point, the Life, Death and Resurrection of Jesus Christ, together with the Third Source, the Prophetic Biblical Scriptures.

Let us begin, because the Night is falling.

PART I
SOURCE ONE:
THE BOOK OF NATURE

THE BOOK OF NATURE

*T*he scientific enterprise as predicted in the prophecy of Daniel has led to an accelerating expansion of knowledge over the past 500 years.

Science, a Christian Endeavor that Compliments the Word of God

In 1952 when I was in the seventh grade one of my teachers gave me a book entitled *One, Two, Three...Infinity* written by George Gamow. It was a wonderful compendium of new research then just coming to the attention of the world, written in the kind of language that laymen could understand. It dealt with the makeup of physical reality. Gamow addressed the idea that the stars of the universe were the engines that made all the elements, including the heavy metals that make life possible on our planet. Gamow was an atheist, but to a believer in God this understanding was an amazing confirmation of how God has made decisions all along the way, detailed wise decisions that made human life on earth possible. This is known as the Anthropic Principle.

When the time came for me to attend Medical school at the University of Washington, I was ready to overdose on the amazing prowess of engineering and elegance that God put into the creation and functioning of the human body and soul. Regardless of the focus, whether through the electron microscope at sub cellular structures or the discovery of the DAA communication and data storage systems that make life flow into every cell and tissue and organ system of the body, the fingerprints of God are everywhere.

Gamow's writings started me on a scientific journey that eventually ended in the twenty first century where amazing agreement between scientific research and Biblical Revelation is clear and unmistakable. The beginning chapters of this book will try to underline this convergence of the scientific world view and the Biblical world view. This convergence will form a compelling backdrop to the divine predictions given in God's Word. This in turn will help the church to understand what is coming rapidly upon the whole world, and the truth that only the church is in a position to help the human race find God's way through the unprecedented desolations that will end this Age. The mounting evidence demands the return to God as the basis of all reality.

Scientific Surprise #1

THE ANTHROPIC PRINCIPLE

The recent sharp focus on the evidence that the universe was designed by God as the place for mankind to encounter Him in time is called the Anthropic Principle. Man is the main feature of creation. Hear the insight of Hugh Ross, in his article entitled "The Anthropic Principle: A Precise Plan for Humanity":

> The anthropic principle says that the universe appears 'designed' for the sake of human life. More than a century of astronomy and physics research yields this unexpected observation: the emergence of humans and human civilization requires physical constants, laws, and properties that fall within certain narrow ranges - and this truth applies not only to the cosmos as a whole but also to the galaxy, planetary system, and planet that humans occupy. To state the principle more dramatically, a preponderance of physical evidence points to humanity as the central theme of the cosmos.
>
> In 1961, astronomers acknowledged just two characteristics of the universe as 'fine-tuned' to make physical life possible. ... By the end of 2001, astronomers had identified more than 150 finely tuned characteristics. ... In the 1960s the odds that any given planet in the universe would possess the necessary conditions to support intelligent physical life were shown to be less than one in ten thousand. In 2001 those odds shrank to less

than one in a number so large it might as well be infinity[4]

For a marvelous detailed chronological presentation of the Anthropic Principle, see Hugh Ross' work *Improbable Planet*.

Scientific Surprise #2

THE ANTHROPIC PRINCIPLE INEQUALITY

The recent discovery of information showing that man is recent and his arrival on earth leaves only a relatively short time until life ends here on the planet, is a big surprise called the Anthropic Principal Inequality. In the groundbreaking book *More Than a Theory*, Hugh Ross discusses the emergence of evidence for this discovery.

> *Brandon Carter, the British mathematician who first used the term 'Anthropic Principle' in the scientific literature observed a stunning temporal imbalance: the universe took billions of years to prepare for a species with the potential to survive no longer than a few million years. Carter called this imbalance between the minimum possible time required for the emergence of human life and the maximum time for humanity's survival the 'Anthropic Principle Inequality.' Physicists John Barrow and Frank Tipler later showed that this inequality is far more acute than originally thought. They calculated that human civilization with the benefits of some technology and organized social structure can last no longer than 41,000 years.*

---

[4] Ross, 2016 entry in Wikipedia

Furthermore, Barrow and Tipler demonstrated that the inequality exists for any conceivable intelligent physical species under any realistic possible life support conditions. "These conclusions were developed, in part, because it takes at least 9 billion years to form a stable planetary system with the right chemical and physical conditions for life. It takes at least another 4.5 billion years for a planet in that system to accumulate adequate biomass and biodiversity to support an advanced civilization's activities. The convergence of 'just right' conditions for an advanced species to thrive and civilize in as brief a time as 13.75 billion years reflects extraordinary, even miraculous efficiency."[5]

In a recent *Reasons to Believe* article, Dr Ross highlighted research on ice cores showing that glacial cycles are **recent fine-tuning** events of the earth that made our present technologic intensive civilization possible including the ability to feed seven billion people. The climate of earth became stable enough only 9,000 years ago to allow the launch of the historic civilization explosion of city building and agriculture and, most recently, technology. This ongoing stable climate is not expected to continue, and the present level of resource consumption cannot last. The last and most extensive Ice Age peaked only 21,000 years ago. The maternal mitochondrial evidence that man is a recent arrival on earth leaves him only limited time to live out generations of brief existence in which to experience Evil and Good and to make a wise decision as to whether to seek and find God his

---

[5] Hugh Ross, *More Than A Theory (Reasons to Believe); Revealing a Testable model for Creation,* p. 114

Creator or live and die without hope or meaning.[6] In short, human history is beginning on planet earth but must find a new heaven and earth if life is to go on. We arrived with time to find God and enter his Kingdom rule but the major living we were created for must find its home elsewhere.

Scientific Surprise #3

ACCELERATING COSMIC EXPANSION

The very recent growing consensus that the universe shell has been expanding in an accelerating fashion for at least the last seven billion years, driven by hitherto unknown Dark Energy, (a self-stretching characteristic of space), is a real big surprise. Add to this the recent observations that this expansion is maintaining a universe that is flat. Change in all of reality is picking up speed for some unrecognized but divinely controlled reason. The surprise here is the word 'acceleration' which points to a basic instability of reality, of cosmic proportion, that is as mysterious as it is unavoidable.

Scientific Surprise #4

DARK MATTER

The recent discovery that over 80 percent of the matter in the universe composing galaxies and star systems is dark

---

[6] Ac 17:26-28

matter held together by gravity, but which doesn't interact with visible matter in other ways. Surprise: could this be heaven? Ingenious recent studies, using the lensing effects of light passing through a strong gravitational field, show the Dark matter to be distributed as filamentous and cloud like structures investing the visible matter in galaxies, thus preserving the galactic structures. Dark Matter and Dark energy seem to make up 95% of all the energy and matter in the universe. **Most of physical reality is invisible!**

Scientific Surprise #5

THE HIGGS BOSON...END OF EVERYTHING SCENARIO

A recent article on the significance of the Higgs Boson, written in *American Nuclear Society*, states:

> *The Higgs Boson, sometimes referred to as the 'god particle', much to the chagrin of scientists who prefer the official name, is a tiny particle that researchers long suspected existed. Its recent discovery lends strong support to the Standard Model of particle physics, or the known rules of particle physics that scientists believe govern the basic building blocks of matter. The Higgs boson particle is so important to the Standard Model because it signals the existence of the Higgs field, an invisible energy field present throughout the universe that imbues other particles with mass. ... Now that scientists measured the particle's mass last year, they can make many other calculations, including one that*

seems to spell out the end of the universe. ...

Here's how Hawking describes this doomsday scenario in the preface of a new book: 'The Higgs potential has the worrisome feature that it might become metastable at energies above 100 [billion] giga electron volts (GeV). ... This could mean that the universe could undergo catastrophic vacuum decay, with a bubble of the true vacuum expanding at the speed of light. This could happen at any time and we wouldn't see it coming.[7]

When very influential scientists like Stephen Hawking and Joseph Lykken are talking about the instability of the Higgs Boson and its field in terms of it changing energy states and thus causing a bubble of annihilation that could end the universe, it gives conceptual support to two New Testament prophetic assertions. John in Revelation 20:11 speaks of the heavens and earth simply disappearing before God's presence:

And I saw a great white throne, and Him that sat on it, from whose face the earth and the heaven fled away; and there was found no place for them. (Re 20:11)

Peter says the same thing in more stark language:

But the day of the Lord will come like a thief. The heavens will disappear with a roar; the elements will be destroyed by fire, and the earth and everything done in it will be laid bare. Since everything will be destroyed in this way, what kind of people ought you to be? You ought to live holy and godly lives as you look forward to the day of God and speed its coming. That day

---

[7] http://www.livescience.com/47737-stephen-hawking-higgs-boson-universe-doomsday.html

will bring about the destruction of the heavens by fire, and the elements will melt in the heat. But in keeping with his promise we are looking forward to a new heaven and a new earth, where righteousness dwells. (2 Pt 3:10-13)

Scientific Surprise #6

THE WORLD IS A SPACE TIME CONTINUUM

The Greek word *aion* has 2 parts to its meaning. A space, meaning world, and a time, meaning Age.[8]

In the past God spoke to our ancestors through the prophets at many times and in various ways, but in these last days he has spoken to us by his Son, whom he appointed heir of all things, and through whom also he made the universe. (He 1:1-2)

From one man he made all the nations, that they should inhabit the whole earth; and he marked out their appointed times in history and the boundaries of their lands. God did this so that they would seek him and perhaps reach out for him and find him, though he is not far from any one of us. 'For in him we live and move and have our being.' (Ac 17:26-27)

Since Albert Einstein published his paradigm changing

---

[8] *A Greek-English Lexicon of the New Testament and Other Early Christian Literature,* Bauer, 1979, U. of Chicago.

thoughts on relativity, we have come to see time and space as a piece. The physical universe is a space time continuum and when spiritual/physical beings die physically they are free to enter a different space time continuum or eternity itself. In these terms God himself inhabits eternity and all of time. The Apostle Paul says it this way, *"We are confident, I say, and willing rather to be absent from the body, and to be present with the Lord."* (2 Cor 5:8)

Scientific Surprise #7

WHAT IS MAN'S SIGNIFICANCE?

Science Has an Existential Setting Begging for Explanation

What is the significance and meaning and destiny for a recently arrived sinful race uniformly experiencing death from generation to generation and untold physical and relational suffering throughout its brief history? In the words of a friend of Socrates, a brilliant philosopher of ancient Athens, in the *Phaedo* written by Plato, one of the greatest philosophers of history, **"we need some sure word from God."**

Scientific Surprise #8

EXPLOSION OF KNOWLEDGE AND TECHNOLOGY

The acceleration of the accumulation of knowledge

and its powerful relative technology is threatening the freedom of every individual and according to some very bright people (Musk, Hawking) will culminate in the production of amoral non-personal machines far more intelligent than us and able to destroy mankind without feeling. This is not a prophecy but a stark warning of where knowledge and technology are leading us today.

A recent report in the Wall Street Journal is hauntingly explicit about the problem of lethal intelligent machines. Note the answers given to Daniela Hernandez by Nick Bostrom, founding director of the Future of Humanity Institute at Oxford University, on the existential risk of AI (Artificial Intelligence). Daniela asks, "How do we decide what values a machine should learn?" Nick Bostrom's answer in part is chilling, "Well, this is a big and complicated question: the possibility of profound differences between values and conflicting interests. And this is in a sense the biggest remaining problem. ... We will conquer nature to an ever-greater degree. But the one thing that technology does not automatically solve is the problem of conflict, of war. At the darkest macro-scale, you have the possibility of people using this advance, this power over nature, this knowledge, in ways designed to harm and destroy others. That problem is not automatically solved."

Earlier in the same interview Nick Bostrom says, "We don't yet understand how general human-level AI (Artificial intelligence) will work or what influence it will have on our lives and economy. The scale of impact is often compared to the advent of nuclear technology, and everyone from Stephen Hawking to Elon Musk to the creator of Alpha Go has advised that we proceed with caution."[9]

Scientific Surprise #9

NEUROPLASTICITY HIGHLIGHTS THE SPIRIT OF MAN

Some 50 years ago, a man found himself rapidly becoming an invalid despite medication and the best thinking of medical science. His illness was called 'Parkinson's disease'. In a moment of inspiration he decided to force himself to walk as fast and as far as he could manage. In time he was walking five fast miles three times a week and, in time, regained drug-free control of his life which lasted into his late seventies. His symptoms regressed to the point that he was released from his Parkinson's support group by well-meaning physicians who believed he never had the disease.

It seems that on his own he had discovered that the spiritual part of his self could order his brain to re-task the healthy parts of itself and support the movement of his body made dysfunctional by the death of dopamine cells in a part of his brain called the *substantia nigra*. Their death results in a lack of dopamine, which is necessary for the cruise control of the nervous system to drive the physical body. Today the treatment of brain disorders has been upgraded by the discovery that the brain can, in the right circumstances, replace neural circuits and even regrow lost cells. The

---

[9] http://www.wsj.com/articles/whats-next-for-artificial-intelligence-1465827619.

regrowth of cells was recently reported in the Mayo Clinic Health Letter for August 2016 about research using exercise to treat early Alzheimer's patients. "The study suggests that increased fitness may help induce the creation of new nerve cells in the cortex, possibly counteracting the effects of neurodegenerative diseases, such as Alzheimer's."

Of course the emphasis on the decision-making spiritual part of man is not fully accepted by many scientists, but the use of *Occam's Razor*[10] in this situation surely leans heavily in the direction of man's spirit directing man's physical body. This is not a new concept to followers of Christ who have seen sin hardened people transformed by God's Holy Spirit daily for two thousand years.

---

[10] The problem-solving principle that "Entities should not be multiplied without necessity."

PART II

SOURCE TWO:

THE BOOK OF HUMAN HISTORY

SOURCE TWO: THE BOOK OF HUMAN HISTORY

The Cross of Christ – true shock and awe – is the central event of human history with no also-rans. The prophetic surprise of all surprises is the historic revelation of who God is through the life, death, and resurrection of Jesus Christ

THE GLORY OF THE CROSS

> *Otherwise Christ would have had to suffer many times since the creation of the world. But he has appeared once for all at the culmination of the ages to do away with sin by the sacrifice of himself. Just as people are destined to die once, and after that to face judgment, so Christ was sacrificed once to take away the sins of many. (He 9:26-27)*

*J*t is hard to understand the thinking of the Devil in moving the authorities to crucify Christ. It would appear as we examine Satan's expectations that he wanted to see God get so angry that He would annihilate the entire race. However, once again he showed his complete ignorance of the heart of God: `

> *You see, at just the right time, when we were still powerless, Christ died for the ungodly.* (Rm 5:6)

It was mid-morning when the Roman soldiers finally arrived outside the city gate and set up shop at the site of their many crucifixions. Three criminals were in their care. Screams of terror and pain pierced the air as the hands of the two terrorists were nailed to their crosses. The third man behaved in a remarkably different manner. As the nails were hammered, he cried out,

> *Father, forgive them, for they know not what they are doing!* (Lk 23:34)

A dying man's last words underline the kind of man he is. This man was dying with one thought uppermost in his thinking:

FORGIVENESS!!!

The three were then lifted up and their crosses dropped into three holes in the ground with three bone dislocating thuds. Surprisingly, the silence was soon broken with a stream of invectives all directed at the man hanging on the middle cross. The words were strange to hear as they criticized the victim for healing, saving, helping others, but now, he needed to save himself. Even the two criminals joined in and advised him that if he indeed had any power, he should use it to save them as well. He was ridiculed for claiming to be God's Son. The Roman governor in a stroke of cynicism and disdain for his Jewish subjects had a placard placed above the central figure that enraged many. It proclaimed:

JESUS OF NAZARETH
KING OF THE JEWS

Presently, one of the terrorists inexplicably stopped making fun of the man. He had obviously meditated on what he was hearing and saw jealousy and a strange irony in what the religious leaders were saying. And of course, he had his own memories of the man as did everyone in Jerusalem. He turned to his partner in crime and said to him,

> Don't you fear God, since you are under the same sentence? We are punished justly, for we are getting what our deeds deserve. But this man has done nothing wrong.

Then he said, "Jesus, remember me when you come into your kingdom." The Lord answered him," I tell you the truth, today you will be with me in Paradise."[11]

What? Something significantly out of the ordinary is in play here. A self-confessed sinner in the process of being judicially executed for his crimes is heard asking a man, who was dying with him, for salvation when he comes into His Kingdom. And the man, without hesitation, tells him that that very day they will be together in Paradise.

Let us be clear here. The criminal is identifying himself

---

[11] Lk 23:40-43

as a willing member of the man's Kingdom. And the man being crucified with him accepts his request. It is important to note that 'Paradise' is used by Paul to speak of the third heaven;[12] it is noted by Ezekiel as the original workplace of the King of Tyre[13], referring to Satan and the mountain of God. It is the promised goal of the victorious Christians in the Letters to the Seven Churches; (Rev. 1-3). Paradise is part of the eternal sanctuary of God.

"Jesus, remember me when you come into your Kingdom."

What a profound insight. Jesus has taken the path of suffering for this very reason. He is the Child born to us; he is the Son given to us; the government will be upon his shoulders. But who will he rule? "For all have sinned and come short of the glory of God;" Rom 3.23. The fallen covering Cherub, the liar of liars, uses his original gift to guard God's holiness to highlight the sinfulness of every man. There will be no kingdom unless God finds a way to restore mankind.

My Father, if it is possible, may this cup be taken away from me."
(Mt 26:39)

God Plans to Die to Save Mankind!

But there is no other way. Father, Son and Spirit agreed on the necessity of the cross before embarking on their Creation work. The End calls for the Cross of Christ. And here he is. The now humbled terrorist is unwittingly actually focusing Jesus on the task at hand. **Unless Jesus**

---

[12] 2 Co 12:2
[13] Ez 28:13

becomes sin for us, bearing the wrath for all sin, and then welcomes us into his death (by our repentance and faith), he will be king of no one. "If anyone would come after me, he must deny himself and take up his cross daily and follow me."

Here is the question. How will anyone follow Jesus into his kingdom if, like the terrorist, they are sinners? The answer is that, like the terrorist, they must die with Jesus as he did. **By faith we die with Christ.** Hear Paul:

> Since, then, you have been raised with Christ, set your hearts on things above, where Christ is seated at the right hand of God. Set your minds on things above, not on earthly things. For you died, and your life is now hidden with Christ in God. When Christ, who is your life, appears, then you also will appear with him in glory. (Co 3:1-4)

Paul again:

> Or don't you know that all of us who were baptized into Christ Jesus were baptized into his death? We were therefore buried with him through baptism into death in order that, just as Christ was raised from the dead through the glory of the Father, we too may live a new life. (Ro 6:3-4)

A little later two people are seen approaching the central cross. Such behavior marks them out as identifying with the victim and a willingness to share in his being cast out of society. One of the people is a young man apparently walking away from a rich inheritance and the other is the mother of Jesus now an older widow who surely has been the focus of long term mean social rejection because of his birth. She is all alone except for her son who is hanging on the cross. Clearly, they were both deciding to identify with Jesus.

The response of Jesus was amazing. He pronounced them a family and they went back into the world in each other's care. Joining Jesus at the cross leads to transformation from a self-centered, broken existence to the ability to be there for others, especially the marginalized. *Noon was approaching.*

Suddenly the sun stopped shining and the entire planet was plunged into darkness. If seen from outer space, the entire solar system was unplugged as it were from the sun. All the taunts and threats and mockery died down. All that could be heard were the sounds of three men trying to take another breath by pushing up on their nail pieced feet. What is going on here?

There are comments in the Astronomical records of the Han dynasty of a day in the Spring of AD 30 when the sun and moon failed to shine. The comments include the explanation that on that day 'the perfect man' died for the sins of the world.

Seven hundred years before, the Prophet Isaiah told us that the Man of Sorrows would face every single sin ever committed, or ever to be committed.[14]

> *We all, like sheep, have gone astray, each of us has turned to our own way; and the Lord has laid on him the iniquity of us all.* (Is 53:6)

For three hours this Lamb of God fights to stay alive so that every sin and all the shame can be made one with himself. He, who knew no sin, is becoming sin for us. Just

---

[14] Alec Motyer, *Isaiah*, IVP

weeks before in the Temple he said to the Jews:

Very truly I tell you, before Abraham was born, I am!" (Jn 8:58)

This man is the only man who could actually face all the sin and suffering of the human race, past, present and future. He is **in** all of time and eternity! He is the Godman. Or, in the words of John the Baptist, the Lamb of God...

...who takes away the sin of the world. (Jn 1:29)

He is the Kinsman-Redeemer of every man who comes to him by faith, the one of a kind sinless Kinsman-Redeemer, capable of taking our place in judgment on the cross.

He too shared in their humanity so that by death he might destroy him who holds the power of death - that is the devil. (He 2:14)

Hours later, when the transfer of sin was complete, he cried out in a loud voice:

"Eloi, Eloi, lema sabachthani?" which means "My God, my God, why have you forsaken me?" (Mk 15:34, Ps 22)

Suddenly, the light returned. This verse is a direct quote from Psalm 22. He is announcing the crisis point of our salvation. He is all alone! God has been wounded as the Father 'forsakes' the Son, who has become sin for us, as the Son bears the full wrath of God against sin. This is an everlasting moment for the Living God, Father Son and Spirit! His abandonment was foreshadowed in the scapegoat teaching of the Torah. Jesus has borne away our sin into oblivion and it is seen and remembered no more. This 'man of

sorrows' bears eternal wounds from the eternal Hell he
entered for us:

> Then I saw a Lamb, looking as if it had been slain, standing at the
> center of the throne, encircled by the four living creatures and the
> elders." (Re 5:6)

Just to solidify the moment for what it was, the man
cries out:

> I am thirsty. (Jn 19:28)

Of course, he is! This is not just the symptom of
hypovolemic shock or a mouth too dry to speak. This is the
testimony of the Son of God who for the first and only time
in his eternal existence is thirsty for God!

**He is experiencing the basic spiritual pathology of
Adam's fallen race.** We are all thirsty for God but don't
know it. This is why this man was crucified in our place; to
bring God back to us. And he succeeded in making that
happen. He knew it. So he cries:

> It is finished! (Jn 19:30)

Then he bows his head and says:

> Father, into your hands I commit my spirit. (Lk 23:46)

His message from the cross began with Father and
ends with Father. Then he breathes his last and dies.

This is the centerpiece of our study of the End. It was
decided by the determinant will of God before the ages were
made[15]. The Age of the Knowledge of Good and Evil could

---

[15] Ac 2:23

not be finished until the Son, by his propitiatory death,
removed the restrictions (The Seals) of the Age. His death
brings the rule of God back to mankind. His death answers
the slanderous words of the Devil about God. His death
vindicates the martyrs. It removes from repentant sinners the
wrath of God. It answers the prayers of the saints of every
generation, "YHWH save us!" His death brings to birth
adopted children of God bearing the loving nature of God.
**His death removes all chance of death and guarantees
unending life for all who trust him.** His death was decided
upon before all else in the Creative plans of God. From the
beginning God knew that true, everlasting freedom to love
within his everlasting Kingdom would demand it:

> *All inhabitants of the earth will worship the beast - all whose
> names have not been written in the book of life, belonging to the
> Lamb, who was slain from the creation of the world.* (Re 13:8)

> *For God was pleased to have all his fullness dwell in him, and
> through him to reconcile to himself all things, whether things on
> earth or things in heaven, by making peace through his blood,
> shed on the cross.* (Co 1:19-20)

1. THE CROSS REVEALS THE TRUTH ABOUT GOD

The Cross reveals the truth about God and puts the lie
to Satan's slander concerning God. The Great War taking
place in the universe is over the true nature of God. The cross
reveals God to be fully engaged with every human being. He
is so present that he enters into all the pain and shame of
mankind. He sacrifices himself for sinners and thus defines
infinite sacrificial love by who he is.

2. THE CROSS REDEEMS SINFUL PEOPLE FOR GOD

The work of Christ, in bearing our sin in our place, delivers us from judgment and cleanses us so completely that the Spirit can come and indwell us. The Spirit's presence changes everything. He is the one who resurrected Jesus from the dead and he promises to resurrect all who belong to Jesus by faith when they die:

> For while we are in this tent, we groan and are burdened, because we do not wish to be unclothed but to be clothed instead with our heavenly dwelling, so that what is mortal may be swallowed up by life. Now the one who has fashioned us for this very purpose is God, who has given us the Spirit as a deposit, guaranteeing what is to come. (2 Co 5:4-5)

3. THE CROSS RESTORES FALLEN HUMANITY FOREVER

The newly restored people bear the image and likeness of God and they must be in free, loving community to accomplish this. The entire universe becomes the dwelling place of God and all repentant mankind are his Kingdom of Priests. This can be stated another way. God finishes his work of restoring mankind and reconciling the Universe. We all step into the Seventh Day. Evil has ceased to be. A New Heaven and Earth comes on the scene united as one:

> Therefore go and make disciples of all nations, baptizing them in the name of the Father and of the Son and of the Holy Spirit, and teaching them to obey everything I have commanded you. And surely, I am with you always, to the very end of the age." (Mt

28:19-20)

Then I saw a 'new heaven and a new earth,' for the first heaven and the first earth had passed away. (Re 21:1)

Then God blessed the seventh day and made it holy, because on it he rested from all the work of creating that he had done. (Ge 2:3)

For my Father's will is that everyone who looks to the Son and believes in him shall have eternal life, and I will raise them up at the last day. (Jn 6:40)

I pray that the eyes of your heart may be enlightened in order that you may know the hope to which he has called you, the riches of his glorious inheritance in his holy people, and his incomparably great power for us who believe. That power is the same as the mighty strength he exerted when he raised Christ from the dead and seated him at his right hand in the heavenly realms, far above all rule and authority, power and dominion, and every name that is invoked, not only in the present age but also in the one to come. And God placed all things under his feet and appointed him to be head over everything for the church, which is his body, the fullness of him who fills everything in every way. (Ep 1:18-23)

Jesus, in John's Gospel, comments on the charge that he broke the Sabbath (by healing a man) by pointing out that both he and his father haven't stopped their work yet:

In his defense Jesus said to them, 'My Father is always at his work to this very day, and I too am working.' For this reason, they tried all the more to kill him; not only was he breaking the Sabbath, but he was even calling God his own Father, making himself equal with God. (Jn 5:7-8)

The last enemy he will address is death, and he will raise all who trust in him on the Last Day, the holy Sabbath, the seventh day in the week of Creation, the day without time boundaries, the beginning of eternity. Further, Jesus tells Martha that whoever lives and believes in Him will never die:

> Jesus said to her, 'Your brother will rise again.' Martha answered, 'I know he will rise again in the resurrection at the last day.' Jesus said to her, "I am the resurrection and the life. The one who believes in me will live, even though they die; and whoever lives by believing in me will never die. Do you believe this?
>
> (Jn 11:22-25)

Matthew reports the resurrection of some Old Testament saints days after the death and resurrection of Christ. This is consistent with the promise to Martha and the declaration of Paul in 2 Cor 5 that resurrection, since the death and resurrection of Christ, is a given for his people at their death. This makes coherent sense if at death we leave this space time continuum and step into eternity with Jesus. After all, the veil was torn when Jesus died and the way back to God is now wide open:

> At that moment the curtain of the temple was torn in two from top to bottom. The earth shook, the rocks split, and the tombs broke open. The bodies of many holy people who had died were raised to life. They came out of the tombs after Jesus' resurrection and went into the holy city and appeared to many people.
>
> (Mt 27:51-54)

Paul in his letters affirms that when a believer leaves his body, he enters the presence of The Lord. He further says that when our earthly tent is destroyed, we have an eternal building waiting for us in heaven. At the cross we die with Christ and are born anew by the Spirit. When we die physically, we are resurrected into glory by the same Spirit. This deep confidence was central to Paul facing death throughout his ministry. **It is the strength of all believers today and it will be the essential confidence of the overcoming Church in the End.**

> *Grace and peace to you from God our Father and the Lord Jesus Christ, who gave himself for our sins to rescue us from the present evil age.* (Ga 1:3-4)

Christ crucified fulfilled the Day of Atonement. From the beginning of time, the Eternal God planned to be united to his adopted family. The Day of Atonement, celebrated in Israel for some 3400 years, underlines this Great Holy Desire of God. He invites all who desire oneness with Him to come and rest in the awesome work of the Lamb of God, Jesus Christ. All who come are indwelt by God himself as Holy Spirit! Atonement was fulfilled at Pentecost!

PART III

SOURCE THREE:

THE BIBLE, GOD'S WORD

SOURCE THREE: THE BIBLE, GOD'S WORD

THE OLD AND NEW TESTAMENTS ARE RICH IN TRUTH ABOUT WHAT GOD PREDICTS FOR MANKIND.

*T*he role of science in understanding the glory of God's creation is very hard to measure. It dazzles the mind. Careful scientific investigation can lead to remarkable applications, such as computers, planes, robotic surgery, stent placement, PET scans, the cloud, Space telescopes, etc. But so far scientific minds have not been able to accurately predict the future. Not that the Marxists haven't tried but so far, the law of unintended consequences has confounded everyone.

Only the One who exists in all time and eternity at once actually knows what is coming in the future. He has demonstrated his ability wonderfully in Holy Scripture.

Let us now move from the wonders of scientific examination, and reflection on the nature of reality, to what God says is still ahead waiting for us in the future.

PREDICTING THE FUTURE IS GOD'S REALM AND THROUGH HIS WORD, *THE BIBLE*, HE HAS GIVEN US PROPHETIC DATA

Prophetic Word #1   Genesis 1:2-8

SCRIPTURE COINCIDES WITH A SCIENTIFICALLY DERIVED SEQUENCE OF CREATION EVENTS.

The Mosaic book of the Genesis Creation account follows the same sequence of appearance and expansion of the universe as the modern Big Bang Inflationary Cosmology. (See Writings of Hugh Ross, *More Than a Theory: The Fingerprint of God*).

Prophetic Word #2   Genesis 1:2-8

NORMAL AND DARK MATTER SEEM TO CORRESPOND TO THE VISIBLE AND INVISIBLE REALMS OF THE BIBLE

The Mosaic book of Genesis hints at the division of matter between visible and invisible early in the creation process.

The Cosmos Has Two Rooms:

And God said, "Let there be a vault between the waters to separate water from water." So God made the vault and separated the water under the vault from the water above it. And it was so. God called the vault "sky." And there was evening, and there was morning - the second day. (Ge 1:2-8)

For in him all things were created: things in heaven and on earth, visible and invisible, whether thrones or powers or rulers or authorities; all things have been created through him and for him. (Co 1:16)

Though outwardly we are wasting away, yet inwardly we are being renewed day by day. For our light and momentary troubles are achieving for us an eternal glory that far outweighs them all. So we fix our eyes not on what is seen, but on what is unseen, since what is seen is temporary, but what is unseen is eternal. (2 Co 4:12)

Now it surely would be easier to skip this point, but it is necessary in order to see how God designed the cosmos. Part of the universe we exist in is invisible to us on planet earth. Paul insists that when the Son made all things, some of them were invisible to us. The throne of God and the power structure of heaven, including the angels and the powers that rule us, cannot be seen by us. He further insists that the visible world we see is temporary, including the visible heavens. Very recent discoveries in the universe identify Dark Matter which is real and five times more prevalent than visible matter as enveloping the Galaxies and is the reason that such huge structures hold together rather than fly apart.

But dark matter is invisible to us. The Genesis account *describes* initial conditions where matter (the waters) is present covered by darkness with the Spirit soaring over it. God divided matter into two parts and called their partition *raqia (Hebrew)*

This has been a point of derision by scientifically minded people and it is usually when the commentators will say the *Bible* is not a scientific text. However, the emerging scientific data of the past few decades is overturning both science and Biblical interpretations of the cosmos. *Raqia* is not a solid dome that forms the sky. It is a separating factor that divides creation into two rooms.   Another recent discovery is that the cosmos is flat in three dimensions and at the same time for the past seven billion years has been expanding without a center in an accelerating fashion because of a self-stretching part of the cosmic space surface called Dark Energy. Further the Scriptures use *raqia* when describing the interface between God's throne and his prophets.[16] It is a profound separation between God's heaven and the rest of visible creation. One practical aspect of this is that, after the cross, Satan and his angels were driven out of heaven down to earth. For two thousand years he and his 'Dark minions' have been ravaging our world though restrained by God. Near the End, the restraints will be removed, and Jesus says radical evil will then attempt to end all life on earth. This simple adjustment of the cosmos by the Creator has made a space where mankind can choose in freedom between life with God or a perilous existence without him.

The division is not permanent. God intends, sooner

---

[16] Ex 24:9-10, Ez 1:26, Ac 1:9, Gn 28:12, Re 4:1

rather than later, to extinguish the present heavens and earth and replace the Cosmos with a new unified heaven and earth. The present arrangement requires worshippers to walk with God humbly by faith. Christ Jesus ascended into heaven 40 days after his resurrection and disappeared. The angels promised that Jesus would return to earth one day just as he left it. This also is consistent with the pattern of the Tabernacle shown to Moses at the top of Sinai in God's presence: a two roomed tent.

When Jesus died on the cross the veil of the Temple was torn from top to bottom, symbolizing that the door was now opened for God to come and indwell his people.

Prophetic Word #3   John 5

THE GOSPEL OF JOHN LENDS SUPPORT TO NON 24-HOUR DAYS IN GENESIS 1.

The Mosaic book of Genesis read in the light of the Gospel of John and the authoritative letters of the Apostle Paul affirms the days of creation are still being played out by God as he finishes making a perfect heaven and earth populated by perfect human beings. The perfection of repentant sinful creatures will occur at death when resurrection will usher them into God's presence in the seventh day, eternity. Specifically, Jesus had much to say about the Last Day in John 5. He answered his critics who said he was not allowed to heal on the Sabbath by saying that his Father was still working to this very day, and he himself was working too. In the context of Genesis 1 & 2, this seems to indicate that we are all still in the sixth day of creation. In John 6, Christ said four times that on the Last Day he would raise his people to life everlasting. He saw this Last Day coming soon when the dead would hear his voice and those who heard would be raised to life. A few days after the death of her brother Lazarus, Martha affirmed that she believed he would be raised to life on the Last Day. Jesus corrected her with these words:

> I am the resurrection and the life. Whoever believes in me even if he dies, he will live again, and whoever lives and believes in me will never die. Do you believe this?" (Jn 11:25)

> Very truly I tell you, a time is coming and has now come when the dead will hear the voice of the Son of God and those who hear will live." (Jn 5:25)

Prophetic Word #4   Gen 2, 3

THE GARDEN OF EDEN

Ground Zero is a Garden with Two Exits

One of the miraculous mysteries of the universe with two rooms is the making by God of a Garden, eastward in Eden, where the invisible and visible are found together as one divine meeting place. Here time seems to be a different entity as the man observes God making living animals and has at his leisure the opportunity to study and know each life form well enough to give names to them. The Garden is a place of nascent possibilities still unformed in the likeness of fruit bearing trees. Two in particular are planted by God in the center of the garden. One tree carries inherently the possibility of sustaining life in unbounded deathless eternity. The other carries a certain death warning along with the intriguing opportunity promised to experience Good and Evil. The very nature of the double experience seems to be the opportunity **to make an informed choice** about the rule of God and the alternative of existence in opposition to God.

The Garden has also the qualities of being a sanctuary where God and the heavenly host can meet two new beings called man and woman. They are beings designed to bear the image of God and to in some capacity act as his regents to rule the life created on the planet. The creation of man from dust and spirit by God and the formation of woman from man's rib, highlights the high and holy community of marriage in their life together. Gender means something. Generational growth meant something long before the rebellion occurred.

This Garden allowed the two to encounter God in all his holiness and goodness and excellence. It also mysteriously allowed radical evil, called the Serpent, to speak slanderous lies in an attempt to gain control of the couple. This being as he appears in Scripture had already caused division and destruction in the universe and though only a created being, to command a following of former angels in God's Kingdom. He is tolerated by God but never poses a true threat to God's sovereign rule. He is amazing in comparison to the couple but not in comparison to God. Why is he tolerated and why is he exercising freedom to oppose God in the presence of God? **This is the mystery of**

Iniquity.[17] But he is not a mystery to God, and he is bounded always by the infinite wisdom of God who bends even rebels to accomplish his ultimate will.[18]

This special Sanctuary becomes the place where the first man will freely choose to join the Serpent in his rebellion. The fallen couple are then driven from God's presence into the room of a part of creation with four dimensions, where entropy rules and where the Serpent will eventually be banished. It is the place from which he will be defeated and cast into Hell with all his angels for eternity.

So, in summary, ground zero for mankind is a Garden with two exits. The Garden symbolizes the Throne of God. The tree of life represents the reality of life forever with the Creator. The second tree will require leaving God's Throne Garden to enter a carefully designed four-dimensional world called earth:

> Now the Lord God had planted a garden in the east, in Eden; and there he put the man he had formed. The Lord God made all kinds of trees grow out of the ground—trees that were pleasing to the eye and good for food. In the middle of the garden were the tree of life and the tree of the knowledge of good and evil. (Ge 2:8-9)

In the Holy Sanctuary of Eden God revealed himself as the powerful Creator God. And Adam discovered himself as a confidant of God who listened to his thoughts and responded to them with respect. God went even further in walking with Adam. He made him into a spiritual community of husband and wife. The essence of two realities had been planted by God in this divinely designed Garden.

[17] 2 Th 2:7
[18] Re 17:17

The story, as it unfolds, reveals the presence of true freedom in which a unique cosmic choice was presented to Adam. He could eat of the tree of the knowledge of Good and Evil, but the consequences would be fatal to him in the end. Or, he could refrain from disobedience and choose to live out of the Tree of Life.

The grace of a needed companion in the life of freedom and choices was provided by God. None of the animals created by God were able to provide this suitable companionship. Indeed, the relationship was holy, mystical and unique. Woman was made of Adam's bone and flesh. The union was pure and secure without a hint of fear. It seems that their bodies and self-awareness was more like what we see saints in heaven to be in Scripture. In Revelation, the righteous dead are pointedly clothed in white raiment and the army of Christ is composed of resurrected saints clothed in white raiment riding with Christ into fallen earth. In heaven, however, there will no longer be male and female distinctions.[19]

Tragically, Eve allowed an alien person in her presence to speak sedition to her, a being called the Serpent. Where was Adam? Their conversation focused on the forbidden tree and its fruit. Indeed, one could say that Eve was already experiencing knowledge from the Evil Serpent. Did she seek out Adam for his help? Apparently, she was fooled by the lies and dazzled by the possibilities of godlessness. She ate from the tree without resistance. Adam, said the Apostle Paul, was not deceived.[20] He, in terrible freedom, took the fruit from

---

[19] Lk 20
[20] 1 Tm 2:14

Eve's hand and ate it. What was he thinking? *Eve diDa't die immediately! Perhaps he thought that the possibility for more to life than dependence on God was worth the risk. The Serpent was obviously opposed to God and still living.* The whole episode was sordid and shallow. In disobedience the couple lost each other and also the protection and comfort of God. Within five minutes, I'm sure they wished they could undo what they had done. Here the awful truth of the realness of life with God is seen. He respects our decisions. They have true consequence. The consequences were not long in coming. The serpent had reason to expect that the couple would be destroyed on the spot. But instead, amazingly, YHWH God Almighty came on the scene with questions.

"Adam, where are you?"

"Who told you that you were naked?"

"Have you eaten of the tree from which I commanded you not to eat?"

"What is this you have done?" (Ge 3:9-13)

God gave his attention next to the Evil One called the Serpent. In the context of a snake God pronounces the curse of falling to the lowest level of existence where he would devour the dust and would die at the hands of a descendant of the woman, the seed of the woman.

To the chagrin of Satan, the LORD God had a plan in place. To the woman he spells out a life of suffering and oppression. To the man, who knew he was doing wrong, he curses the ground. Outside the Garden the earth would disappoint him and prove to indeed be cursed. It seems that Adam and Eve exited Eden **into the height of the last Ice Age.** God announces that life will be very hard for Adam until he finally dies physically and returns to the dust. Entropy reigns! He emphasizes a play on words with Adam's name. Adam's name, 'dusty', had been a gentle ongoing warning that apart from God that is all he is.

By God's grace, Adam is able to help heal his wife by lovingly naming her Eve, 'the mother of all the living,' and life continues for them at a very feeble flame.

YHWH God clothes Adam and his wife with garments of skin, a far cry from their spiritually alive condition before they sinned. God must clothe them with a 'working sense of self' that will lift them from hopelessness and suicidal depression, so that they can go on living. In his work *The Meaning of Persons*, Dr Paul Tournier calls this gracious provision 'the human personage.' This provision is far less than what God ultimately plans a person to be, but it allows life to go forward in a world infused with evil and deception. He places them out of reach of the Tree of Life so that their predicament does not become eternal.

However, he graciously leaves them in sight of the way back to the Tree of Life by placing Cherubim to guard the way back with a flaming sword. Elsewhere, the Cherubim cry "Holy, Holy, Holy is YHWH of Hosts" and most likely they sang this message for thousands of years near Eden until the flood obliterated the way back to the garden. God, from the start, is the God of all hope. His resources are limitless. Something profound is in the works. Obviously, God has not given up on mankind. God, in his wisdom, is planning to use the catastrophe of human sin to accomplish His own loving gracious ends.

For Adam and Eve, the Age of the Tree of the

Knowledge of Good and Evil has begun, and it will give all mankind a painful unforgettable experience of Evil. The tree was designed by God. The space time continuum in which it resides was designed by God as a room where existential decisions about God and truth could be made in freedom. It is true that Jesus says we are all born slaves of sin, but, as the Spirit strives with our hearts over time, we are given opportunities to turn to God in repentance. These encounters with God are real and planned by God.

Many years ago a high school student in the far Northwest province of the People's Republic of China, called Xinjiang, reacted to the daily message from her schoolteachers that God didn't exist, and life was a matter of Evolution, by asking herself why they drummed this into their heads every day? Much of what they said turned out not to be true, so she looked at the creation around her and came to the conviction that God the Creator did indeed exist. However, she didn't know him. One night as she looked up into the night sky, she said this, "God, I know you are there, but I don't know you. Please show yourself to me." Months later she traveled to the ancient city of Xian to attend university. There her American English teacher told her class about how she found Jesus Christ to be her life and Lord. Ruth came up afterwards and thanked the teacher for telling her God's Name and right there surrendered her life into his hands. She encountered new birth by the Spirit of God and her entire life took on meaning and hope and joy.

So, the Age of Evil was permitted by God. With the permissive will of God, the rebels lived on in time, though always on borrowed time. The reality of Good and Evil they experienced was made possible by God in his inscrutable wisdom. **Good and Evil came from his hand, symbolized by his planting a second tree in the center of the Garden next to the Tree of Life.** So, mankind entered a world where all would learn by experience both Good and Evil as the two temporarily coexist. Casting its shadow over all, as well, was the deeply held conviction of God concerning terrible freedom. Freedom, an integral part of God's image, is a gift he gives to Adam's fallen race. The process of saving sinners involves God graciously empowering them in time to freely choose to repent and yield to God. The question this Age raises is: can God make a universe of free moral, loving creatures who will remain together, obedient and humble, in God's ruling presence in all the Ages of eternity? From the start of Creation, the Living God knew that such a Kingdom would only be possible by his full disclosure of himself at the cross, giving his creatures full experiential knowledge of Evil and then giving them a new redeemed nature. This Age would see the Cross of Christ occur and, through it, bring about perfect sons and daughters for God and, best of all, the utter End of Evil.

> *In the past God spoke to our ancestors through the prophets at many times and in various ways, but in these last days he has spoken to us by his Son, whom he appointed heir of all things, and through whom also he made the universe. The Son is the radiance of God's glory and the exact representation of his being, sustaining all things by his powerful word. After he had provided purification for sins, he sat down at the right hand of the Majesty in heaven. (He 1:1-3)*

> *In bringing many sons and daughters to glory, it was fitting that*

God, for whom and through whom everything exists, should make the pioneer of their salvation perfect through what he suffered. Both the one who makes people holy and those who are made holy are of the same family. So Jesus is not ashamed to call them brothers and sisters. (He 2:10-11)

Prophetic Word #5   Genesis 1, 11

GENESIS 1-11 IS FINDING MUCH CONFIRMATION IN RECENT STUDIES ON GLACIERS, LANGUAGE, HUMAN MIGRATION AND EXPLOSION OF CIVILIZATIONS

Very recent scientific studies have begun to establish the veracity of the Mosaic stories of early mankind including: the Noahic flood, the lability and proliferation of language, the explosion of civilizations after the onset of the present unprecedented stable interglacial period, and the populating of the earth in rapid fashion. Even the great ages of early man and the reduction to present ages correlate with the radiation from a super nova at just the right time.[21]

The present explosion of civilization occurred substantially after the flood, which seems to be linked to events of the last glacial age. Apparently, the climate of the last glacial age was hostile to civilization's progress, holding back agriculture and city building. It is possible that early generations of modern man were sheltered in the Eden Basin, where substantial structures would have been covered by the flood. Genesis chronicles the total degeneration of the race

---

[21] See Hugh Ross's profound book, *Navigating Genesis*

prior to the flood, including long periods corresponding to the ancient myths of demigods and human heroes. This time could have spanned much of early man's 100,000 to 50,000 years of existence.

Prophetic Word #6   Genesis 3:15

GOD PROMISED THAT ONE MAN WOULD COME AND GIVE THE SERPENT A MORTAL BLOW

Moses wrote that humanity would need a Savior from the power of the Serpent (radical evil). The Savior would come through the 'seed of the woman,' and that this seed would also come through an historic ancestor of Abraham. Isaiah and Micah promised that the Savior would come through a virgin, be born in Bethlehem, and grow up near Galilee of the Nations. Jesus was born of the virgin Mary of the lineage of David, in Bethlehem. Jesus grew up in Nazareth and, once and for all, defeated Evil and saved Mankind at the cross. Revelation 12 describes the post Cross confrontation with the Serpent and his humiliating exit from heaven. Christ did indeed prepare a place for us. The final demise of Evil will occur at the end of this Age.

Prophetic Word #7   Isaiah 13-27

THE PROPHETIC SEER, ISAIAH, SAW IT WILL BE FAILED GOVERNMENTS TO THE END

The Prophet Isaiah appears in the reigns of Uzziah, Jotham, Ahaz, and Hezekiah, kings of Judah. His Prophecies cover the period from 739 BC to the present. He was the quintessential Seer of old. He was given the ability to see the human struggle to cope with survival in a world torn by evil right through to the End of the Age.[22] There he saw the last civilization on earth, which he characterized as the 'city without meaning' as it was being destroyed. **These earth rending desolations are interrupted by the coming of the glorious Messiah, and the perpetrators of destruction are arrested by God.**

Isaiah has an astounding record of prophetic success. He predicted the incarnation of Jesus. His servant songs document Christ's saving ministry. He predicted the Babylonian captivity and its ending at the hands of Cyrus the Persian. He talks about a time of righteous rule over the whole earth by the Christ. He predicts a New Creation of Heaven and earth by the LORD. His haunting words were used by John the Baptist to introduce himself as "a Voice crying in the wilderness" and Jesus of Nazareth as 'the Lamb of God' who will save mankind from their sins and as the one who would pour out the Spirit on God's people.[23]

Isaiah's most penetrating vision is elaborated in Isa. 13-27. Alec Motyer has a very good analysis of these chapters in his devotional *Isaiah By the Day*. Hear the words of this great Isaiah scholar as he comments on Isa 24:10:

> *The city of meaninglessness has been broken up. 'Meaninglessness' is translated from tohu (Hebrew), which Gen. 1:2 uses to describe*

---

[22] Is 13-27
[23] Is 40, 53, 61.

the material substrate of creation before the Creator gave it shape, order, light, life and meaning. Jeremiah (4:23-26) uses the same word when he sees creation under judgment, bereft of light, stability, living creatures, ordered growth and organized society. Isaiah sees the world as a city (man's greatest effort at organized society), where 'nothing adds up' and where, under judgment, everything comes crashing down—like Babel, humankind's first city with its meaningless gabble and its unfinished tower (Gen. 11:1-9).[24]

Prophetic Word #8   Daniel 9:26

THE PROPHET DANIEL SAW IT WAS WAR ALL THE WAY TO THE END

The Prophet Daniel appears in history at one of the lowest moments in the story of the Jewish people. Their leadership was apostate. The nation had stumbled into the orbit of the Babylonians while looking for a place of honor among the nations sans their God YHWH. Daniel and other royal teenagers were taken as hostages and possible eunuch ministers of state for King Nebuchadnezzar in 605 BC. Daniel and his friends decided to keep themselves loyal to their God and to the best calling of an Israelite. But they did this as they lived among the nations and proclaimed again and again the glorious truth about YHWH (Yahweh), the covenant God of Israel, to those peoples.

---

[24] *Isaiah by the Day*, note 6 of 24:10, page 120.

In 530 BC[25] Daniel heard God say to him that a great war was going on between God and Radical evil. It concerned the truth. The war would cover this entire Age until God brought it to an end. Further, this faithful prophet saw the redemptive history of Israel as 70 weeks of years. The first 69 centered on God's Anointed coming and dying to accomplish a perfect salvation for sinners without establishing a physical kingdom. Then Jerusalem and the temple would be destroyed, and the end would come like a flood, war will continue until the end, and desolations have been decreed.[26]

We now know that a hiatus of at least 2000 years has occurred when Israel was again exiled among the nations. The absent nation Israel reappears in 1948.

Prophetic Word #9   Daniel 9:20-27

IN THE MIDDLE OF WEEK 70, THE FINAL BEAST WILL PLACE AN ABOMINATION IN A TEMPLE AND DESOLATION WILL ALMOST ENGULF THE EARTH.

Daniel tells us that during the 70th week, a very evil man will defeat the people of God. He will make a covenant with many, break it in mid-week, cause an abomination to be seen in the temple, and then attempt to destroy the world by unparalleled desolations. In the midst of this carnage, the Son of Man will return and make an end of the Beast and establish God's people in an everlasting Kingdom of God.[27]

---

[25] Dn 10:1
[26] Dn 9:26
[27] Dn 7:8-14; 8:9-14; 9:27; 11:36-45; 12:1-4

The salient points of these five references are included by Jesus in his sermon on the Mount of Olives.[28]

Prophetic Word #10   Daniel 7:13-14

DANIEL SEES A HUMAN BEING RECEIVE UNIVERSAL WORSHIP

The premier truth found in Daniel's prophetic writing is his reference to 'the Son of Man,' who will defeat the Evil One, save God's people from sin and persecution, and will give rule over the Kingdom of God, including worship. In Jesus' day the name 'son of man' could be a sign of humility, a sign of basic humanity, the nation of Israel's true coming redeemer 'God in the flesh.'[29] Jesus fills the full meaning of all three definitions!

Unlike the unbroken line of flawed prophets and leaders, Jesus suddenly appears at just the right time, the perfect Son of Man.

Prophetic Word #11

Ps 22, Is 53, Da 9, Mc 5:2

JESUS OF NAZARETH, BORN OF MARY, CAME INTO THE WORLD FROM ETERNITY

---

[28] Mt 24, 25; Lk 22; Mk 13.
[29] Is 9:6

The Eternal Son of God, Jesus of Nazareth, in 6 BC entered human history, born of the virgin Mary, as predicted by Isaiah. He overcame sin in the flesh, in the world, and from radical evil. Once perfected by what he suffered, he yielded himself to be crucified on a Roman cross by sinful men, becoming one with the sin of every man (past, present, and future, for he is the Great 'I Am'). Then, he experienced the full isolating wrath of God in our stead. This was surely an eternal event, symbolized by the eternal wounds he bears for all to see. All this was seen by King David, Isaiah, and then Daniel as written in the Old Testament.

Prophetic Word #12   John 14, Rev 12

JESUS' DEATH STOPPED THE ACCUSATIONS OF SATAN IN HEAVEN AND MADE A PLACE THERE FOR ALL BELIEVERS

In the upper room on the night he was betrayed, Jesus told his disciples that he would be going on ahead without them. They should not be troubled, since he was going to prepare a place for them at his Father's side. When he had finished his work, he would come for them personally and take them to be where he was. When asked how, he said, "I am the way, the truth, and the life. No man comes to the Father except through me." The next day he died on a Roman cross, was buried, and on Sunday morning rose triumphant from the dead. Jesus told his disciples that this glorious offering would prepare a place for them at the Father's side, and that he would come for them and take them to where he lived in the bosom of the Father.[30] This accomplishment of Christ is described in detail in Revelation 12, where Satan, the accuser of the brethren, is cast out of Heaven down to earth. There he is opposed by Christians who triumph over him by the blood of the Lamb and by the word of their testimony, and by the fact that they did not love their lives so much as to shrink from death."

Prophetic Word #13

Jn 5:1-30; 6:39, 40, 44, 54

JESUS EXPLAINS THE INTERFACE BETWEEN TIME AND ETERNITY...AS DAY 7 FOLLOWS DAY 6 OF GENESIS 1, 2.

Jesus had much to say about the Last Day in John 5. He answered his critics (who said he was not allowed to heal on the Sabbath) by saying that his Father was still working to this very day and he himself was working too. In the context of Genesis 1 and 2, this seems to indicate that we are all still in the sixth day of creation. In John 6, he said four times that on the Last Day he would raise his people to life everlasting. He saw this Last Day coming soon and said it had already come when the dead would hear his voice and those who heard would be raised to life. A few days after the death of her brother Lazarus, Martha affirmed that she believed he would be raised to life on the Last Day. Jesus corrected her

---

[30] Jn 1:18; 14:1-6

with these words, "I am the resurrection and the life. Whoever believes in me, even if he dies, he will live again, and whoever lives and believes in me will never die. Do you believe this?"[31] The evangelist Matthew reports in his Gospel[32] that at the moment of Christ's death, an earthquake occurred. The veil in the Temple was torn, the rocks split, and the graves of some godly people were opened. When Jesus rose from the dead, they were also resurrected and were seen walking through the city of Jerusalem. Thus, the Last Day seems to correspond best with the eternal seventh day, which in Genesis 1 is not bracketed by 'it was evening and morning.' It stands for eternity, as opposed to our space-time continuum which we leave at our death to take our place in eternity with Christ. So, at death, which indeed happened to everyone in the upper room, Jesus came for them and took them to his Father's side. In Paul's words, "to be absent from the body is to be present with the Lord."

Prophetic Word #14

Da 9:26; Mt 24:2; Mk 13:2; Lk 21:6

JESUS PREPARES HIS DISCIPLES FOR THE DESTRUCTION OF THE TEMPLE AND ITS REPLACEMENT BY THE CHURCH

Jesus had much to say about the end of the Age. Days before his death, he taught his disciples that a great

---

[31] Jn 11:25
[32] Mt 28: 51-53

revolution in redemptive history was about to be accomplished.[33] The physical Temple building was soon to be destroyed as predicted by Daniel. This was a point made by Jesus to the Jewish leaders when he said to them in John 2, "Destroy this temple and in three days I will raise it up again."[34] They deceptively brought this up at his trial to show his hostility to the Temple Building. Jesus was indeed the Temple through the miracle of the Incarnation and after his work on the cross made it possible for the Spirit to come and indwell believers. We now know Herod's temple ` was replaced by the Church on Pentecost circa 30 AD, when the Spirit entered the 120 believers at prayer in the Upper Room.

The plan was simple yet elegant. The one venerable building was replaced over time by millions and millions of believer's bodies, alone and in community. Jesus promised them that when the Spirit was given as promised they would become his witnesses and carry him into the farthest reaches of the world. The plan, simply stated, is that the Church would literally be the visible representation of Christ in the world and in eternity;[35] Thus, it should not surprise us that the Church must play a central role in the End when her suffering obedience will set the stage for an unprecedented harvest of souls at the coming of Christ.

> *And God placed all things under his feet and appointed him to be head over everything for the church, which is his body, the fullness of him who fills everything in every way.* (Ep 1:22-23)

---

[33] Mt 24, Lk 22
[34] Jn 2:19
[35] Ep 1:22-23

Prophetic Word #15

Mt 24:4-5; Mk 13:5; Lk 21:8

JESUS WARNS US THAT LIES AND DECEPTIONS WILL INCREASE AS THE END APPROACHES

The first concern of Jesus for his apostles is that they understand that their adversary is a master liar. The world ahead would be filled with deception. This is unquestionably the major problem of the twenty-first century. The following list is representative but not exhaustive.

First, we have the old deceptions from the beginning of the Age:

- ✓ God is not enough
- ✓ Human effort must be united for human benefit
- ✓ God is like us and his rule is thinly veiled selfishness
- ✓ Children have little value

Later near the time of Christ we have the following deceptions:

- ✓ Might makes right
- ✓ Matter is eternal
- ✓ People are commodities
- ✓ God is beyond knowing even if he actually exists
- ✓ Smart men are the measure of truth.

And, seven centuries into the battle:

✓ God is not a Father

✓ Jesus didn't die on the cross

✓ There is no Trinity

And, finally, today:

✓ Life is the result of spontaneous self-organizing generation

✓ There is no true truth

✓ Truth claimers are the real oppressors

✓ Human rationality is suspect

✓ Feelings and good stories trump evidence

✓ Human government exists to provide for all human needs

✓ Statism replaces divinity

✓ What you see is all there is

✓ Man is not exceptional among the animals

✓ Man can control the planet

✓ Progress is taking place

✓ Scientism usurps divine worship

✓ Thousands of false religions & utopian prophets.[36]

---

[36] Author's own list

Prophetic Word #16

THERE WILL BE INCREASING PERSECUTION OF GOD'S PEOPLE, CULMINATING IN MASSIVE MARTYRDOM IN THE END

Jesus warns us that we would be present as wars, natural disasters and catastrophes happened in the run up to the End. He warned that wickedness would increase so greatly that the love of most would grow cold. But, in spite of the rise of evil causing dwindling numbers of believers, some would stand and proclaim the Gospel of the Kingdom in testimony to all the nations and only then the End would come:

> *Then you will be handed over to be persecuted and put to death, and you will be hated by all nations because of me. At that time many will turn away from the faith and will betray and hate each other, and many false prophets will appear and deceive many people. Because of the increase of wickedness, the love of most will grow cold, but the one who stands firm to the end will be saved. And this gospel of the kingdom will be preached in the whole world as a testimony to all nations, and then the end will come.* (Mt 24:9-14)

Prophetic Word #17   Acts 9:1-18

THE APOSTLE PAUL AN APOSTLE OF LOVE, BEGAN AS THE ENEMY OF CHRIST[37]

Paul walks onto the stage of human history as a legalistic Pharisee intent on destroying all memory of a crucified Christ. His conversion to be an Apostle of Christ ranks second only to the resurrection of Christ as proof of the truth of the Gospel. He was martyred circa 65 AD in Rome by beheading.

Prophetic Word #18   Rom 8

PAUL TELLS US THAT ALL ALONG THE WAY TO THE END, THE PRELUDE TO OUR GLORY WILL BE SUFFERING

Paul, the Apostle of Christ to the Nations, in 35-65 AD writes about the suffering predicted for the church. For them, suffering is the prelude to being glorified with Jesus. Paul says that the suffering will be far outweighed by the glory to follow. Paul says the Church must see itself as Christ's body, given to evangelize the world as a dying sacrifice of lambs; cf Rom 8. Using himself as an example, he says this evangelistic suffering is a joyous completing of the full story of Christ's suffering for his body which is the

---

[37] Died a martyr in 65 AD

Church.[38]

Prophetic Word #19   Eph. 6:10-20

CHRIST IN US EQUIPS US TO STAND TO THE FINAL END

Paul the Pastor spoke to the church, pointing out that we are not fighting human beings but powerful, highly placed Evil. We must not deal with these powers on our own. We must put on God himself as our armor. With him we can expect to stand in the day of Evil and thus to overcome what evil sends our way. And, most importantly, we must pray on every occasion with every kind of prayer for all God's people to speak and live with holy boldness. In the words of Major Ian Thomas, "All there is of God is available to the one who is available to all there is of God!" His Book *The Saving Life Of Christ*, is a must read for all Christians.

Prophetic Word #20   2 Thess. 2:1-17

THE CHURCH WILL BATTLE THE MAN OF LAWLESSNESS

Paul the prophet warns us that before Christ returns, we must deal with the 'Man of Lawlessness.' He will be a man of lies and satanic miracles who will claim to be God. He will succeed with those who have refused to love the

---

[38] Co 1:24

truth because God will give these foolish intellects a delusion so they will believe the lie.

There are many candidates for delusions these days. First is the delusion that mankind is the result of blind chance, and thus has no meaning or significance beyond simple chemistry. At the time Paul wrote, Evil was under divine restraint, but in the end when this restraint is removed, literally all Hell will break loose. We should understand that the demons? behind recent utopian movements were all wildly successful in killing large numbers of people and destroying large tracts of land. The original tempter was a serpent. All along the corridors of time, Anti-Christ figures appear under his satanic guidance. People like Sennacherib, Tamerlane, Attila the Hun, Genghis Khan, not a few false religious leaders, Hitler, Stalin, Mao, the Caliph of ISIS, etc. But so far, none have won control of the world.

Prophetic Word #21   Romans 8:18-39

IN THE END THE CHURCH, EVER EMPOWERED BY THE LOVE OF CHRIST, WILL BE OFFERED AS SHEEP FOR SACRIFICE

Paul the theologian does not support the idea that the Church will be raptured out of the world before the tribulation. He instead said that we have not only been given the privilege of believing in Jesus but also have been given the privilege of suffering for his Name.[39] And, of course, we must look hard and long at the ending verses of Romans 8:

> *What, then, shall we say in response to these things? If God is for us, who can be against us? He who did not spare his own Son, but gave him up for us all—how will he not also, along with him, graciously give us all things? Who will bring any charge against those whom God has chosen? It is God who justifies. Who then is the one who condemns? No one. Christ Jesus who died —more than that, who was raised to life —is at the right hand of God and is also interceding for us. Who shall separate us from the love of Christ? Shall trouble or hardship or persecution or famine or nakedness or danger or sword? As it is written: 'For your sake we face death all day long; we are considered as sheep to be slaughtered.'*

> *No, in all these things we are more than conquerors through him who loved us. For I am convinced that neither death nor life, neither angels nor demons, neither the present nor the future, nor any powers, neither height nor depth, nor anything else in all creation, will be able to separate us from the love of God that is in Christ Jesus our Lord.* (Rm 8:31-39)

---

[39] Ph 1:20

JESUS TO JOHN
THROUGH HIS ANGEL

REVELATION LIGHT

THE CHURCH IS CRUCIFIED WITH CHRIST

*T*he church is surprisingly God's weapon of incarnate light in the world's last night. Now it is time to pull back the curtain on the part of creation we can't see because it is either invisible or future.

Revelation Light #1

Blessing Upon Proclaimers   Rev. 1:1-3

Jesus himself pulls the curtain back and shows us the eternal invisible realities that will determine the End of the Age. It is published in the New Testament as THE BOOK OF REVELATION. It was shown to John by the angel of Jesus and written down by the Apostle for us. The fact that Jesus sent his angel to tell John was because the Glory of the

Risen exalted Christ was more than John could have endured. John is clear that the blessing that every believing human heart hungers for is given to those who will take the Revelation and proclaim it aloud to people walking in the darkness of death worldwide.

> *The revelation from Jesus Christ, which God gave him to show his servants what must soon take place. He made it known by sending his angel to his servant John, who testifies to everything he saw—that is, the word of God and the testimony of Jesus Christ. Blessed is the one who reads aloud the words of this prophecy and blessed are those who hear it and take to heart what is written in it, because the time is near. (Re 1:1-3)*

Revelation Light #2

Note the Time Factor   Rev. 1:1-3

"What must soon take place" and *"because the time is near"* gives no hint that 2000 years and counting will intervene. The blessing promised for all who read and take to heart what is written is tied to 'the time is near'. The Lord intends to end this specially designed Age of time, and transfer from it his newborn children. Literally 'from time into eternity' means that each believer is within less than one normal life span from being with Christ in eternity. Here in time he brings many sons and daughters into existence and at death, or his visible return, into his presence. Jesus promises that all who live and believe in Him will never die. The simple implication of this promise is that at the point of death, Jesus appears; and through the Spirit that raised him from the

dead, he raises his people to everlasting life. Rom 8:11

The unveiling message of this book must be read with this truth in mind. Jesus is himself the resurrection. He promises to personally come and take his people to His Father's bosom.[40] Paul says it this way: "When we absent the body, we enter his presence. There we are swallowed up by life." (2 Co. 5:1-10; Ph.1:23)

Revelation Light #3

This Rich Unveiling of the Future is the Spirit of God Talking About Truth in All its Fullness

This divine unveiling of reality is a unique display of several genres of literature. Its title declares it to be 'apocalyptic', unveiling truth as powerful symbolic visions, creatures, and many episodes of warfare and battles. It is at times strongly 'prophetic', like the prophets of Israel, exposing sinful behavior and calling for the righteous to come out of this corrupt generation before judgment follows. Parts of it seem like 'pastoral letters' dealing with specific matters in various church communities. Part of it is just glorious 'worship' and profound celebration at the promise of God's personal presence in an entirely new, united universe. But the really unique message of the book is its 'Lordly call' to the church to participate in the final battle of God against the powers of darkness as he brings about the greatest harvest of souls in the history of the Age. As the angel who

---

[40] Jn 1:18; 14:6

was leading John around said to him, (when John fell at his feet to worship him):

> Don't do that! I am a fellow servant with you and your brothers and sisters who hold to the testimony of Jesus. Worship God! For it is the Spirit of prophecy who bears testimony to Jesus. (Re 19:10)

All churches, engaged in serving Christ by obediently Preaching the Gospel of the Kingdom as a testimony to the nations along the way, will have to speak about the details of The End of this Age and point to the Age to come. We are equipped by this amazing word of Jesus to take our place with the heavenly messenger host in engaging evil in our world. Jesus made this clear when shortly after his resurrection he announced that he now had all the authority in heaven and on earth and was sending his disciples to make disciples out of the formerly pagan nations of the world. And he specifically promised us his personal presence here, not to the rapture but to the end of the Age. The indwelling Christ makes the Church, His Body, the final power structure to be reckoned with by Evil. **For why else would we be in His Right hand with His Spirit?**

Revelation Light #4

Who is God?   Rev. 1:3-18

John is full of wonder and the Spirit as he opens us up to join in the journey into the invisible part of reality and the future at the invitation of Jesus. He is literally going to heaven and back; along the way we will see 'behind the scenes' of human history as it unfolds to the End. He will address the people of God, symbolized as seven churches in the province of Asia (arguably the center of the Church at that time). He brings us grace and peace from the three he saw in the center of God's throne. They are God the Father, the Sevenfold Spirit, and Jesus Christ the Eternal Son. The One God is hyper-personal.

He then pours out praise and adoration for Jesus: faithful witness, the firstborn from the dead, the ruler of the kings of the earth, the one who loves us, our liberator from sin through his blood, the Creator of a kingdom of priests to serve his God and Father; to him be glory and power forever and ever; (Age after Age).

"Look he is coming with the clouds!" (Re 1:7)

The Lord God says, "I am the Alpha and the Omega. Who is, and who was, and who is to come, the Almighty." Because John decided not to feel sorry for himself or for the churches, he recognized the honor of serving God. The suffering, the Kingdom and the patient endurance were a privilege we all share.

Rev. 1:10: "I heard behind me a loud voice like a trumpet, which said:

"Write on a scroll what you see and send it to the seven Churches found in the Province of Asia."

"Someone like a son of man" (Re. 1:13) was walking among seven lamp stands appearing as a Glorious Eternal King before whom John a former disciple fell down as a dead man. "Then he placed his right hand on me and said: "Do not be afraid. I am the First and the Last. I am the Living One; I was dead, and now look, I am alive for ever and ever! And I hold the keys of death and Hades." Here then we have the full picture of who God is. With God unveiled we see that the present and the future are in good hands. Clearly Jesus sent his angel to speak to John because the transcendent glorious Christ overwhelmed John's fallen humanity.

Revelation Light #5

THE CHURCHES

What is the Church?

Revelation 1:19-20

*T*he churches are the ordinary communities of an extraordinary Christ Jesus with real addresses in the world (this present Evil Age). The seven churches of the Province of Asia are symbolic of the miraculous outposts of the Kingdom of Christ on their way together through the whole world.

The glorious Risen Christ has seven stars in his right hand (the seven stars are the messengers of the seven churches). In the words of Jesus "all power in heaven and on earth has been given to me, therefore go and make disciples of all the nations ... And surely I am with you always to the very end of the Age."[41]

Indeed, drawing back the veil shows us Christ Jesus standing among seven lamp stands which "are the seven churches." So the picture is coherent. The light from the lamp stands are seen as stars in the darkness of the world.[42] We must not miss the symbolism by thinking of guardian angels, pastors or evangelists. The Master Jesus is living in and walking in the midst of his churches and speaking to the messenger, and with his right hand (all powerful) he is empowering these messenger churches to light up the darkness by living out together the message of the Gospel of the Kingdom. They are expected to live such compelling lives that the nations will choose to decide to follow Jesus. We must not think that churches have angels attached who will speak on their behalf. In the seven letters to the churches Jesus talks directly to each church and says: "Whoever has ears, let them hear what the Spirit says to the churches."

Churches that light up the world have a common characteristic: they listen to the Word of God.

---

[41] Mt 28
[42] Ph 2:15

Revelation Light #6

MESSAGE TO THE CHURCHES

What is the Message to be Lived Out?

 ## THE EPHESIAN MESSAGE

Revelation 2:1-7

TAKE NOTE "You have forsaken the love you had at first... If you do not repent, I will come to you and remove your lampstand from its place."
"To the one who is victorious, I will give the right to eat from the tree of life, which is in the Paradise of God."

During Christ's ministry John heard him pray to the Father:

"I have made you known to them and will continue to make you known in order that the love you have for me may be in them and that I myself may be in them." Jn 17:26

During the end of John's ministry the church would carry him on a bed to the front of the congregation in Ephesus and he would get up on his elbow and say: **"Children, love one another."** Over John's life as an Apostle, he understood that the supernatural indwelling of the Church by Christ brought the greatest power in the universe, **the love the Father has for the Son** and placed it in the Church.[43]

A few years ago a purse was snatched by some children during our prayer service. Our church is in the city of Milwaukee in a neighborhood that was called 'Little Beirut' before we moved in. Fourteen crack cocaine houses operated within two blocks. Blessed Trinity, the Catholic church whose building we purchased, had once been the busiest church in Milwaukee. So, The Gangster Disciples marked our buildings. Cars were chopped up in the school yard and our large parking lot was the drug drop center of the area. Despite the problems, our church grew as an urban/suburban servant fellowship, and the high crime rate descended to a very nominal rate. The reason: fear drove us to serious daily prayer and the Spirit filled us with His love.

Back to the purse, when this happens my modus operandi is to immediately walk into the neighborhood behind our church and talk with the mothers and grandmothers in charge. Having accomplished this with kind reception by the ladies, I noticed a party was in progress a

---

[43] Jn 17:26

block away. About forty 18-25-year-old men were gathered. I noted that it was very dark, but I introduced myself and told them of the theft with the caveat that I was not looking for suspects but wanted them to talk to the younger kids about the evil of stealing from a church.

Their response was awesome. After loudly underlining the heinousness of the theft, which they pointed out that no self-respecting gang member would do, they promised to have a heart-to-heart talk with the kids. There in the darkness I responded with, "Thanks men, we love you," to which immediately all forty young men said, "And we love you too." This was not superficial banter, as most of those young men participate in Saturday morning basketball (in our new gym) and discipleship with committed men of our fellowship. 'Little Beirut' is becoming a Christ-altered community.

 ## THE SMYRMNA MESSAGE

Revelation 2:8-11

Paraphrasing this message: "I'm the eternal God, and I died and came to life again. In other words, I've made the journey you are about to take! Note this: you are rich in spite of affliction and poverty. So, do not be afraid of what you are about to suffer...poverty, slander, prison, persecution, death...I will give your life as your victor's crown. The second death will not hurt you at all." We must be prepared to light up the darkness by suffering and dying without fear or unfaithfulness, before a terrified world. One question often asked concerning the book of Revelation is: Does the book speak to the Church down through the Age or is it just focused on the End? A short review of church history answers the question.

> How can we account for such devastating reversals as the annihilation of the church in North Africa, the crushing of Catholic missions in Asia, and, above all, the strangulation of the faith in the Middle East? (7-8th, 12-15th, and 7-21st centuries, respectfully).[44]

The 20th Century alone saw millions of believers martyred in Nazi Germany, the Soviet Union, Maoist China, Ottoman Turkey, and Islamic Northern Iraq. And who can classify honestly the millions who died in the religious wars of Europe over several centuries (15th-17th)? A common thread in all the killing was an acute absence of love by Christians for other Christians, intentional neglect of ethnic communities in the hinterlands, a cultivation of the wealthy and ruling class (that eventually fell out of favor) and strangely, the Christian communities that found common cause with Muslims and Mongols against other Christian communities (i.e. the Coptic Church joined Muslim invaders against their own Byzantine brothers).

So the War against Christians is Age-long, but the culmination of all persecutions will occur when the restraint is removed from Radical evil and it succeeds for a short hour to rule the entire planet.[45] With this caveat, the Church will testify so powerfully before being martyred that a vast

---

[44] Jenkins, John Philip (2008-10-16). *The Lost History of Christianity* (p. 250). HarperCollins. Kindle Edition.
[45] 2 Th 2:6-7

portion of mankind will repent and choose Christ at the siGe of his coming. So the call to obedient angelic ministry will accelerate as the night falls when no man will work!

 ## THE PERGAMUM MESSAGE

Revelation 2:12-17

Note this! Satan has his throne where you live. He has a long history of leading God's people into immoral lifestyles that end in death and snuff out their light in the darkness. Jesus warns at the start that "because of the increase of wickedness, the love of most will grow cold".[46] He links this with the Kingdom imperative of preaching the Gospel as 'a testimony' to the nations just before the End. Such a testimony must demonstrate victory over pornography, lust, adultery, and immorality of every kind. Start your counterattack with My Sword, the Word of God that silences the tempter and spiritually empowers all who are armed with it. Repent, or Jesus will come and fight against those sinning with the word of his mouth. Light up your neighborhood by true intimacy with God and powerful satisfaction with his relational provision and abiding presence in you.

---

[46] Mt. 24.12

THE THYATIRA MESSAGE

Revelation 2:18-25

Start with this... Jesus Christ is Holy and will not tolerate Christian leadership that teaches or practices immoral behavior. Note well the name Jezebel. She was Queen in Northern Israel. She taught as truth that the sexually perverted were just another flavor of life and should be fit into the community of God's people. Her Baal shrines and Asherah shrines replaced the holy worship of YHWH with heterosexual and homosexual religious priests/prostitutes. Sex and alcohol replaced the Holy Spirit as the driving force of life in Israel. Be unpopular if you must, but take a stand for holy love, holy service, and holy faith. Know for sure that the coming millennium that will follow My return will be merciless in suppressing immoral behavior in the world. And to those who refuse to give in to this outrage, I promise you will be given authority over the nations and you will rule them with an iron scepter and dash them to pieces like pottery. In addition, you will light up your dark neighborhood with Hope (the Morning Star) by bringing healing to the victims of this false religion.

THE SARDIS MESSAGE

Revelation 3:1-6

Note this ... the Son gives us Spirit to release the light of life into his people. No one can be an alive-Christian without Spirit. So, talk cannot replace actual life and you folks are dead. Christ sees unfinished attempts to live but nothing actually happens. Wake up and meet Holy Spirit. Let Him in on all your aspirations to live like Christ. Without him you will not understand what is ahead and the signs of my coming. Yet, there are a few in your community who are actually alive.

They will be able to walk with me as resurrected saints. Their names will remain in my Book of the Living Ones and I will acknowledge that you are mine before my Father and his angels.

 ## THE PHILADELPHIAN MESSAGE

Revelation 3:7-13

Note... Jesus is the Ultimate successor to the shepherd and king, David. As the God/man, Jesus is utterly holy, without peer. Who else could justifiably say: 'I am the truth'. As the great Shepherd, he can open doors and gates that matter, like the door into God's presence and the way through death itself. See, the entire world is before you waiting for you to be the weak, human, people of God who shine and walk for only one reason. Jesus commends them, saying: you obey my word and refuse to deny my Name. Any people who claim to be the people of God and deny my Name are not in touch with the truth. Those liars will sooner or later have to confess that I, the God/man, love you, my people.

When will this happen? Most likely when Christ comes back at the last battle, and his followers become martyrs when they meet the Satanic followers of the beast.

Jesus continues his Philadelphian message: I will allow an hour of trial to come on the whole world to test the inhabitants of the earth. But you, my people, are loved by me and have kept my command to endure patiently. And so, I will keep you from the hour of trial.

Friend, think about these words of Jesus Christ: "I am coming **soon.**" All the generations of the churches like Philadelphia died! Jesus came to them and took them to his side in eternity. 'Soon' refers to his coming at their death. His promise to write his Father's name, the name of the city coming down out of heaven, and 'my new name,' puts them squarely in the military levy of the 144,000 who were sealed by the Spirit with the name of the Father and the Son. They are those who, in the Last battle, were martyrs and became the first fruits of those who came out of the Great Tribulation.[47]

And best of all .... when all the dust settles you will find yourselves to be Pillars in the New Jerusalem which is coming down out of heaven to start the New Evil-Free Age.

 ## THE LAODICEAN MESSAGE

Revelation 3:14-22

Take Note: this is how true, faithful, witnessing works.

---

[47] Re. 7:14

Jesus is the answer to all the promises of God. Thus, he is The Amen! Because He is living in the church, the church can deliver His true, faithful witness concerning God. The church becomes a living Amen to all the promises of God. But Jesus now says to the Laodiceans, "You have a problem. <u>Your deeds have no passion in them, for or against God</u>. You say, "Look how rich we are! We have no needs. What can God do for us?" <u>Actually, you are wretched, pitiful, poor, blind and naked!</u> You need three things from me: gold refined in the fire so you can be rich, white clothes to cover your shame and nakedness, and salve for your eyes so you can see. Simply put, you need to experience suffering that forces you to experience my grace making you **rich in knowing me**. You need to be clothed with me to overcome your guilt and obvious spiritual deadness. And you need to be enabled through the Spirit's presence to see God as he is.

If you are at all interested, because I still love you, I am this moment standing outside your community, knocking on the doors of your hearts, waiting for you to invite me in. Open the door and you will begin a life of fellowship with me, feasting at my table. Listen and respond. Turn back to me and receive my rebuke and discipline. Gain the victory over your godlessness, and I will give you the right to sit with me on my throne, just as I was victorious and sat down with my Father on his throne.

My father was a pastor and when he was in Bible school in 1925, he heard a story about a man in Norway named Jan that changed his life. I enjoyed hearing my dad preach and he often told the story of Jan. This Norwegian boy was born number fourteen in a large family. It became apparent to his mother early on that the little guy was slow to learn things. His parents were old, and they wanted to establish him in a way that he could care for himself when they were gone. So they sent him to work as a gardener on a nearby estate. The lady of the estate was a sweet Christian and she would read Bible stories to Jan each evening before he went to sleep in his little gardener's cottage. He loved the Bible stories and soon began to beg her to teach him to read. So, she began the task of teaching him even though he struggled to remember words. He was so determined that after a few years he could read the Bible himself. The lady bought him his own Bible and soon he was reading it himself each night. As he gardened, people would greet him as they passed by.

He always asked them how they were doing, and when they asked him how he was doing he stopped and told them what he had been reading the night before. Soon people would share their hurts, fears, and difficulties. In his simple way he replied, "I will pray for you." It wasn't long before passersby realized that when Jan prayed, God heard him and touched their lives. These encounters continued for years until everyone in the region knew Jan and came to experience Christ in their busy lives. In 1919 the flu pandemic that killed millions of people in the world came to their village. Their beloved gardener of prayer became ill. The women of the village took turns caring for him. They said, "Now we will see how a man of God dies." They were right. When the time came for his funeral service there were no churches large enough for the service. So many people came whose lives had been changed by Jan! He was a good example of what Christ expects of his Church. Christ held

Jan in his right hand and made him a bright light in his village.

As usual, this is the Spirit speaking to the ears of the people of God, getting them ready for 2000 years of the greatest witnessing adventure a human being can have. Near the End, these messages will be the means of raising up a special levy of servants to witness the Gospel of Jesus into the darkness.

Revelation Light #7

WHAT DOES THE KINGDOM
OF GOD LOOK LIKE?

Revelation 4:1-5:14

*W*hen Jesus began his ministry he said, "*The time has come. The kingdom of God is near. Repent and believe the good news.*"[48]

This **revelation was given** a few decades after the barrier between Heaven and earth was opened by Jesus. John saw the functioning Kingdom of God. The purpose of the vision was to show John what must take place 'after this'. All creation in Heaven is aligned in obedience and responsibility before the One who sits on the throne. **Now God has decided to address the situation of fallen man still living**

---

[48] Mk 1:15

in this present Evil Age. God is after all the One who was, and is, and is to come. The entire core leadership of God's Kingdom is present and in worship mode affirming that He is worthy to receive glory and honor and power by virtue of His having created all things. In the Gospel, Jesus said that this willingness of God to reclaim and restore all things is 'Good News', and that fallen mankind must repent and place their trust in the coming Kingdom; Mark 1:14. Strangely no angels are in this power picture, possibly reflecting the rebellion ongoing in the angelic host right on up to the Cross.

The scene now changes, from being centered on the One sitting upon the Throne, to being focused on the right hand of him who sits on the throne (Rev. 5:1), holding a scroll written on both sides and sealed by seven seals.

The story of Adam's race is long and sad. **The divine limitations placed on it will not allow life in all its fullness to occur.** Everything is mixed with evil and ends in failure and death. All through this Age, no one was found who could remove the seals from the story of man or the rebellious universe. John, a very spiritually astute man, realizes what is at stake. Who can redeem the future for mankind? John weeps as the history of total leadership failure seems irreversible. Then one of the elders said to John:

> *Do not weep! See, the Lion of the tribe of Judah, the Root of David, has triumphed. He is able to open the scroll and its seven seals.*

This Triumph is unique to Jesus Christ. He is the 'Arm of the LORD" (Isaiah 53) who redeemed mankind from sin and the just wrath of God by his death on the Cross. (see

PART II). This amazing work of redemption silenced the accusations of the Devil in Heaven and made it a "place for the redeemed to gather out of this Age of Evil'; John 14. It further qualified repentant sinners to become temples of the Holy Spirit and together to become the Holy Body of Christ. And at his resurrection and ascension Jesus arrived in the center of God's throne where in the words of Paul,

> *Therefore God exalted him to the highest place and gave him the name that is above every name, that at the name of Jesus every knee should bow, in heaven and on earth and under the earth, and every tongue acknowledge that Jesus Christ is Lord, to the glory of God the Father.* (Ph 2:7-11)

Here we literally see the entire un-fallen heavenly host come together around the throne of God after seeing in the death of Jesus the glorious truth about who God really is:

> *Then I looked and heard the voice of many angels, numbering thousands upon thousands, and ten thousand times ten thousand. They encircled the throne and the living creatures and the elders. In a loud voice they were saying: "Worthy is the Lamb, who was slain, to receive power and wealth and wisdom and strength and honor and glory and praise!" Then I heard every creature in heaven and on earth and under the earth and on the sea, and all that is in them, saying: "To him who sits on the throne and to the Lamb be praise and honor and glory and power, forever and ever!" The four living creatures said, "Amen," and the elders fell down and worshiped.*

Again in the words of Paul, "all there is of God was in

Christ bringing the universe back together again."[49]

---

[49] Co 1:19-20

Revelation Light #8

THE LAMB UNDOES THE POWER OF THE TREE OF THE KNOWLEDGE OF GOOD AND EVIL

Revelation 5:6; 6:17; 8:1-5

"It is for freedom that Christ has made you free," Paul tells the Galatians.[50] He echoes the promise of Jesus to his disciples and Jewish leaders, "If the Son makes you free you shall be free indeed."[51]

> *You are worthy to take the scroll and to open its seals, because you were slain, and with your blood you purchased, for God, persons from every tribe and language and people and nation* (Re 5:9)

---

[50] Ga. 5:1
[51] Jn 8:36

All Creation was made subject to frustration by the Creator:

> ...in hope that the creation itself will be liberated from its bondage to decay and brought into the freedom and glory of the children of God. (Rm 8:21)

So it is only fitting that the sealed contents be introduced for all to see by the Living Creatures, Cherubim-like beings who guard the holiness of God.

 *Seal #1*

A White horse and a rider is seen with bow and crown who rides out like a conqueror bent on conquest. Now government is a common grace of God and rulers are his servants. So the horse is white because their calling is of God. But the story line of man is one of fallen people riding out to win a kingdom to rule. The best of people fall short in the event of rule and all fail to win control of the world. In the process there is constant war, endless broken promises and many casualties. The sum of the whole enterprise is a loss. "All who came before me, said Jesus, were thieves and robbers"; John 10:8. So why did Jesus succeed where all others failed? He made it possible for sinful, fallible people to become new creations in eternity. He made them *to be a kingdom and priests to serve our God, and they will reign on the earth."*[52] Jesus makes Kingdom people who become in God's hands the building blocks of the New Jerusalem. Yes, our citizenship is in heaven.

---

[52] Re 5:10

 *Seal #2*

A fiery red horse and a rider is given power to take peace from the earth and to make people kill each other. To him was given a large sword. Red is the color of the Dragon and his Beast and his City of Evil, Babylon. This is the impediment of all impediments to peace on the earth, this is Radical Evil eventually cast out of heaven and given, near the end, leave to devour the dust of the earth, mankind. Jesus comes and carries his own out of the Kingdom of Darkness into his Kingdom of Light. We are called to stand in the day of Evil wrapped up in the armor 'of God'; and having done all, to stand. (cf Eph 6:10) Christians stand against evil of every kind, corporate and individual: racism, hatred, slander, murder, lust, pride, etc.

 *Seal #3*

A black horse with its rider is seen holding a pair of scales in his hand. Again, appropriately, a voice from among the Living Creatures says,"2 pounds of wheat for a day's wages, and 6 pounds of barley for a day's wages and do not damage the oil and the wine." God told Adam, "cursed is the ground because of you". The survival of mankind is still a perilous affair made doubly worse by mankind's selfish nature. Not a small percentage of people face starvation because of a lack of concern for others by their fellow human beings. Jesus says to his disciples at the start of his Sermon on the Mount:" Blessed are those...begging for the Spirit, hungry for things to be right, who love mercy and have single-minded hearts for God..."; Matt. 5. God will now do a lot better for them than others have done up until now." Christ makes takers into givers. "Seek first the Kingdom of Heaven and all the rest will come to you as well; Matt. 6:33." Through the gift of Christ's righteous nature, new birth is given to hungry saints. (cf John 3:3)

 *Seal #4*

A pale horse! Its rider was named Death, and Hades was following close behind him. They were given power over a fourth of the earth to kill by sword, famine, and plague and by the wild beasts of the earth. The world is a cemetery where accidental or premeditated death can strike at any moment. This is one of the many reasons that the middle name of Mankind is 'anxiety' (Sartre). The Devil keeps man in bondage to the fear of death because he has been given the power death over mankind. (cf Heb 2:14-15) Praise God that Jesus has replaced the fear of death for his people with the certainty of life. *"And this is the promise that he himself has given us, the promise of eternal Life"[53] and "Whoever lives and believes in me will never die!"[54]*

 *Seal #5*

I saw under the altar the souls of those who had been slain because of the word of God and the testimony they had

---

[53] 1 Jn 2:25

[54] Jn 11:26

maintained. They called out in a loud voice, "How long, Sovereign Lord, holy and true, until you judge the inhabitants of the earth and avenge our blood?" This reminds us of how long this cry has been going up to God...The Lord said, "What have you done? Listen! Your brother's blood cries out to me from the ground."[55] A great damper on progress in this violent world is because of what happens to truth tellers. They are strikingly absent in this Age and this will continue, apparently in accelerated fashion, as the End of the Age approaches. (Note: Christ's warning in the Olivet Discourse; Matt 5-7.) Praise God that Jesus comes at death for his martyrs and will come early to stop the final destruction of life on Earth near the End. For example, when the Bolsheviks took power in Russia, some estimates say that 28 million Orthodox Christians died.

 *Seal #6*

There was a great earthquake. ....

> "Then the kings of the earth, the princes, the generals, the rich, the mighty, and everyone else, both slave and free, hid in caves and among the rocks of the mountains. They called to the mountains and the rocks, "Fall on us and hide us from the face of him who sits on the throne & from the wrath of the Lamb." Rev 6:15-16 NIV

Moses, in Psalm 90, says that Wrath is the atmosphere

---

[55] Gn 4:10

we all live under. Paul says we see the wrath of God falling on godless men who suppress the truth. Jesus says that those who refuse to acknowledge him "abide under the wrath of God." All along the way, God has brought divine wrath on his enemies; for example, the Flood, Sodom and Gomorrah, Babylon, WWII, universal mortality, etc.

Jesus at the cross experienced the wrath of God in our place. Without this unparalleled act of self-sacrifice, no one would have a future. Who can stand in the day of his wrath? Only those who have run to Him for salvation.

 *Seal #7*

There was silence in heaven for about half an hour.

In this Age of the knowledge of Good and Evil **one restriction stands out as pure grace:** we are invited to come to God in prayer for his help in time of trouble. In fact this is actually the only resource given us to cope with the serious problems in our fallen world. The silence symbolizes the amazing lack of prayer rising from the human race. The brother of Jesus, James, tells us that we have not because we ask not. And when we do we ask amiss; (James 4:1-3).

But all of Heaven is tuned to the prayers of God's people. The setting of silence is ominous... The trumpets, announcing the desolations that are about to be turned loose on earth by the Beast, are about to be sounded. Prayer is needed. An angel with a golden censor came and stood before the altar. He was given much incense to offer with the prayers of all God's people, on the golden altar before the throne of God

The smoke of the incense, together with the prayers of God's people, went up before God from the angel's hand. Then the angel took the censer, filled it with fire from the altar, and hurled it on the earth; and there came peals of thunder, rumblings, flashes of lightning and an earthquake. (Re 8:4-5)

Jesus has opened wide to God's people the ultimate resource, prayer. It releases the power of God into our desperate situations down on earth. That is why in places of rising persecution in our world today, prayer movements are springing up. As the darkness gathers and the coming night when no man will work approaches, God's wise people are praying. One set of teaching says this:

> Pray for the destiny of your nation
> Pray for God's will alone to be done
> Pray together

Summary:

> We see God
> We see The Church
> We receive his light messages for God's people
> We see the structure of the Kingdom
> We see the Cosmos reconnected around the Lamb
> We see how Christ reverses the divine restrictions.

Revelation Light #9

THE CHURCH MOBILIZED BEFORE THE STORM

Revelation 7:1-8

*W*hen seal seven was opened by Jesus, it became obvious that the greatest restraint on the human race is the wrath of God. He never retired from our world and intervenes whenever he chooses to make history flow in the direction he wills. The final scene of wrath calls forth a practical question: The great day of their wrath (from the face of him who sits on the throne, and from the wrath of the Lamb) has come, **and who can withstand it?** The answer is encouraging to say the least. God plans to raise up an army equipped to stand in the coming darkness by being sealed on their foreheads as servants of our God. An army with the mind of Christ!

Four angels are seen standing at the four corners of the earth holding back the four winds of the earth to prevent any wind from blowing on the land or on the sea or on any tree. The four angels had been given power to harm the land and the sea, but not until the 144,000 troops from the tribes of Israel had been sealed.

Who are these angels? They seem to be the instruments of the Dragon kept under God's sovereign restraint until the time of desolation is to begin. The list of tribes is unique by leaving out Dan and Ephraim and adding Joseph. The reference to the tribes raises many questions but it must be taken as encouragement to see that God plans to restore Israel to the church in a powerful role at a critical time near the End. For in Christ, God has made Israel and the Gentiles one new humanity:

> Consequently, you are no longer foreigners and strangers, but fellow citizens with God's people and also members of his household, built on the foundation of the apostles and prophets, with Christ Jesus himself as the chief cornerstone. In him the whole building is joined together and rises to become a holy temple in the Lord. And in him you too are being built together to become a dwelling in which God lives by his Spirit. (Ep 2:12-22)

Not only did Jesus bring, through the Cross, the universe together around himself (as seen in Chapter 5) but the church is there as one new humanity as well. This army of Christ will surely add depth of meaning to the promise made to Abraham long ago:

> I will make you into a great nation, and I will bless you; I will make your name great, and you will be a blessing. I will bless

those who bless you, and whoever curses you I will curse; and all
peoples on earth will be blessed through you. (Ge 12:2-3)

This angelic church force will function all the way to
the end and become the first fruits of people offered to Christ
as his martyrs, as stated in Rev 14:1-5. These servants have
the Name of the Father and the Son on their foreheads. They
have been given the attitude of the Father 'who spared not
his own Son' as a part of their mindset and the attitude of the
Son who "refused to be God for himself" but for others. This
advance guard will overcome evil in three ways: First, by the
blood of the Lamb; second, by the word of their testimony;
and third, by not loving their lives so much as to shrink from
death.[56] Their faithful proclamation and deaths will bring
forth new believers from every nation, tribe, people, and
language standing around the throne and around the elders
and the four living creatures. They fell down on their faces
before the throne and worshiped God... ...no one could count
this crowd. (Expert Hugh Ross says that the numbers in the
Greek language could count to hundreds of millions but not
more. So this group of new believers could possibly be in
excess of billions of souls.) Both groups are hard to identify,
indicating that they are in some sense the same group. One
carries the name of Israel, God's people, and the other carries
the name nations, God's people. It is only fitting that this
End of Days Harvest be seen in the context of the promised
blessing to earth through Abraham. Our God is glorious and
faithful and full of love. He knows the stench of evil and sees
what seems to be a world on the brink of Hell. But he knows

---

[56] Re 12:11

what must be done and he is even now working to form this spiritual army of saints with a message and an attitude. The elder knows that this is a defining vision that John must understand. These people have been saved during the great desolating tribulation. God allows the Dragon to do his worst and uses it to accomplish the redemption of a vast number of people:

If those days had not been cut short, no one would survive, but for the sake of the elect those days will be shortened. (Mt 24:22)

Immediately after the distress of those days 'the sun will be darkened, and the moon will not give its light; the stars will fall from the sky, the heavenly bodies will be shaken.' Then will appear the sign of the Son of Man in heaven. And then all the peoples of the earth will mourn when they see the Son of Man coming on the clouds of heaven, with power and great glory. And he will send his angels with a loud trumpet call, and they will gather his elect from the four winds, from one end of the heavens to the other. (Mt 24:22, 29-31)

Revelation Light #*10*

THE DESOLATION OF CREATION

Revelation 8:1-9:21; 11:14-1

his is a sharp shift in subject. In Chapter 6, the theme is the Wrath of God which will be the final word on this present evil Age, replacing this 'sealed Age' with the Kingdom of his dear Son. Chapter 7 is the final word on God's plans to redeem a significant part of the human race as he proves faithful to his promise to Father Abraham to bless the families of the earth through his seed; Gen. 12. Chapter 8 begins with the great throne of God's Grace which has always been the resource of God's people who are encouraged to come and pray and not be discouraged. And in the time of desolations the church will stand in the darkness and pray with every kind of prayer on every occasion for all God's people and see the power of God released against evil on their behalf. "And pray for me," says the great Apostle Paul "that I, whenever I speak, words may be given me so that I will fearlessly make known the mystery of the Gospel, for which I am an ambassador in chains. Pray that I may declare it fearlessly as I should."[57] The desolations about to be announced by trumpets are the result of the restrainer of evil stepping back and allowing for one hour the final Anti-Christ and his ten cohorts to unleash destruction on the human race and its last great civilization. The great rebel will in the end simply do what the Creator wills to be done. Destroy Babylon! Jesus gives his disciples perspective in the Olivet Discourse!

> So when you see standing in the holy place 'the abomination that causes desolation,' spoken of through the prophet Daniel—let the reader understand— then let those who are in Judea flee to the mountains. Let no one on the housetop go down to take anything out of the house. Let no one in the field go back to get their cloak.

> How dreadful it will be in those days for pregnant women and nursing mothers! Pray that your flight will not take place in winter or on the Sabbath. For then there will be great distress, unequaled from the beginning of the world until now—and never to be equaled again. (Mt 24:15-21)

Here Jesus speaks boldly about the unleashing of destruction in concert with the Anti-Christ setting up the abomination predicted by Daniel and Jesus. This time of destruction is shortened and interrupted by the return of Jesus described in Rev. chapter 1. The metaphor of trumpets in the hands of angels seems to indicate that the world is

---

[57] Ep 6:18-20

being warned to flee to God for safety. This would be an appropriate message for the church, battling the Beast, to proclaim. "This Man of Lawlessness plans to end life on the planet. <u>Run to Jesus!</u>"

A few years ago I was asked to encourage a group of Syrian refugees in Jordan, mostly Muslims, who were gathered to receive food and basic gifts to help them cope. I talked to them about **Jesus, the refugee in Egypt and his tender heart for all refugees.** I especially felt the presence of the Holy Spirit when speaking with them that night. I encouraged them in this way: whenever they found themselves awake and afraid in the dark, to call out his name, Jesus! and he would surely come and help them.

First Trumpet

Desolation on the way

Revelation 8:6-7

> Then the seven angels who had the seven trumpets prepared to sound them. The first angel sounded his trumpet, and there came hail and fire mixed with blood, and it was hurled down on the earth. A third of the earth was burned up, a third of the trees were burned up, and all the green grass was burned up.

The first four desolations seem to be uncreating creation; (Elul). Permission from God seems to underlie the desolations. The final woe will come directly from God at Christ's return. One third of the earth, trees and all the green grass burned up by hail and fire mixed with blood hurled down on the earth. The dynamics seem to be that of a maniac being turned loose to destroy creation. This is California wildfires writ large, very large. One third of the earth burned up is a step towards total desolation. Think of the cities and nations crushed by the first stroke of desolation. In July 2014 the TV program *60 Minutes* presented an expert who said that volcanic eruptions could kill millions with little warning. He felt that the greatest danger is posed by Mount Vesuvius in Italy. He also noted that if the Dome under Yellowstone National park erupted as it did 400,000 years ago it would destroy a significant part of North America. Expert Hugh Ross writes in a weekly paper that on average there are extinction events on the planet every 26 million years. So this kind of event has happened many times in the past. But this one comes from the Beast.

The past three decades have been a time of destroyed cities. The author personally saw the cities of Beirut and Mogadishu completely destroyed by civil war in the early 1990's. These city-crushing civil wars are even now swallowing the cities of Iraq and Syria. The number of refugees is the highest now (2016) since WWII.

 *Second Trumpet*

Desolation of the Oceans

Revelation 8:8-9

> *The second angel sounded his trumpet, and something like a huge mountain, all ablaze, was thrown into the sea. A third of the sea*

turned into blood, a third of the living creatures in the sea died, and a third of the ships were destroyed

Hail and fire are followed by something like a huge mountain, all ablaze being thrown into the sea. Again the results are desolation. Does the seer see a mushroom cloud or has radical evil diverted an asteroid to fall on planet earth? The results are immediate and apparently irreversible. What is the time frame? This destruction, like the first, was held up so that the 144,000 could be recruited and discipled to prepare the Christian forces of the Kingdom to battle the beast. The destruction is restrained as the full weight of intercessory prayer is factored into the equation. The harvest of souls is seen so we can all see the travail of the world and church and be satisfied. One third of the sea is dead, many creatures die, and many ships are destroyed. World commerce is mortally wounded. The global village civilization is facing starvation and anarchy and despair.

Third Trumpet

Re-directed asteroid?

Revelation 8:10-11

> *The third angel sounded his trumpet, and a great star, blazing like a torch, fell from the sky on a third of the rivers and on the springs of water— the name of the star is Wormwood. A third of the waters turned bitter, and many people died from the waters that had become bitter.*

The cities, forests and meadows are burning; the sea

and its commerce is hopelessly disrupted; bloody hail, a falling mountain of fire, a great star blazing like a torch continues the motif of a world in flames. The fresh water supply is targeted, and the star is called Wormwood. Here it is noteworthy to remember the breakdown of the nuclear reactor in Chernobyl, in the former Soviet Union, and the loss of life due to radiation for years afterwards. And most mysterious at the time means 'wormwood'. A third of the drinking water has become deadly. Even now potable fresh water is becoming dearer worldwide.   Surely when the Antichrist reaches for the instruments of desolation, he will not hesitate to use chemical, biologic and nuclear weapons. Is this also a metaphor for the loss of truth and reason; and a flood of lies and false feelings...all orchestrated by powerful evil? In that case, this fire has already consumed more than a third of truth.   When Jesus says that no life would survive these desolations unless the time is cut short, he is implying that the time of desolation must be months not years. Even today the fresh water supply is being degraded by pollution and waste.

Fourth Trumpet

The lights go out

Revelation 8:12-13

> *The fourth angel sounded his trumpet, and a third of the sun was struck, a third of the moon, and a third of the stars, so that a third of them turned dark. A third of the day was without light, and also a third of the night.*

If this is leaning at all toward literal, then it makes sense that the world on fire would leave the atmosphere polluted and opaque. The plants and oceans are failing to renew the air. The Anti-Christ is not planning to establish a utopia on earth; he is just waiting for the opportunity to destroy everything. He has some ten allied Kings to use and like a caged lion he will burst forth to destroy as soon as the restrainer is removed. Jesus is showing the heart of the beast so that the battle against the beast will have content and context. It will be a time of months and they will be shortened. *Immediately after the distress of those days 'the sun will be darkened, and the moon will not give its light; the stars will fall from the sky, and the heavenly bodies will be shaken.'* Mt 24:29 NIV

The loss of sun, moon and stars may also point to the disruption of an ordered sense of time, seasons and holidays. The sense of the myth of progress is fading fast.

As I watched, I heard an eagle that was flying in midair call out in a loud voice: "Woe! Woe! Woe to the inhabitants of the earth, because of the trumpet blasts about to be sounded by the other three angels!"

Three very significant difficult times are pointed out as the destructive work of Evil is announced. They are three woes and they are associated with the last three trumpets.

🎉 Fifth Trumpet

First woe - Desolation of hope

Revelation 9:1-11

The fifth angel sounded his trumpet, and I saw a star that had fallen from the sky to the earth. The star was given the key to the shaft of the Abyss. When he opened the Abyss, smoke rose from it like the smoke from a gigantic furnace. ... They were told not to harm the grass of the earth or any plant or tree, but only those people who did not have the seal of God on their foreheads. ... They were not allowed to kill but only to torture them for five months. And the agony they suffered was like that of the sting of a scorpion when it strikes. During those days people will seek death but will not find it; they will long to die, but death will elude them. ... They had as king over them the angel of the Abyss, whose name in Hebrew is Abaddon and in Greek is Apollyon (that is, Destroyer).

The association of this attack with Apollyon (Destroyer) makes the link to the Abomination (that brings desolation) of the Antichrist very probable. But this devastating work of evil is still under the control of God. People sealed by God cannot be harmed. The people tormented cannot be killed. The wounds will last only five months. Remember this is still the Age of the knowledge of Good and Evil. The Abyss, which has been the repository of demons is opened up and earth is inundated with evil unclean spirits. Emotional torment is the feature of this woe and the experience will be educational for many. This will be a wakeup call to many godless people to seek God and live. And a wakeup call for the church, the people who can and will cast out the demons. World-wide depression will cause world-wide psychomotor slowing, suicidal ideation and complete loss of self-worth. Paul warns the church about this:

Don't let anyone deceive you in any way, for that day will not come until the rebellion occurs and the man of lawlessness is revealed, ... at the proper time. For the secret power of lawlessness is already at work; but the one who now holds it back will continue to do so till he is taken out of the way. And then the lawless one will be revealed, whom the Lord Jesus will overthrow with the breath of his mouth and destroy by the splendor of his coming. (2 Th 2:3-8)

Remember, the name of this angelic rebel is "Destroyer". This helps us align what is happening with the words of Paul, Jesus, Isaiah and Daniel. The prophet Daniel predicts Israel's historic experience of Antiochus Epiphanies as a type of Anti-Christ or beast. Jesus makes it crystal clear that Antiochus is not the final Anti-Christ but that when the final man appears, he will cause unprecedented planet killing desolation. This is especially frightening when we think of the array of weapons he will have at his disposal. It is also instructive to see large numbers of former Muslims leaving their faith because of the denouement of the true nature of this religion where it has total control. The people of earth have been deeply discouraged but not killed. Clearly seeing Evil is the preliminary to the clear understanding of the salvation offered in the Cross of Christ [see Matt 24 ref. above]

The advice of the Lord is for those in Judea to run for the hills when the abomination is seen. He is not talking about the final work of the Anti-Christ. He is talking about the need for God to shorten the time so that the destruction of the world is not total. Satan is defeated. He has no hope of escape from the judgment of God. He is full of rage, and when the restraint is removed from him, he will move to destroy the earth. For a short time he will have access to every weapon system, and he will use them:

> In the middle of the 'seven' he will put an end to sacrifice and offering. And at the temple he will set up an abomination that causes desolation, until the end that is decreed is poured out on him. (Da 9:27)

The question must be answered. "What is meant by the Temple and the offerings and sacrifices?" Reading Paul and understanding the reason for the Olivet Discourse points to this being in some twisted way 'a use and abuse' of the Church that will stop its effective resistance to the Evil One and her availability to the Lord as a living sacrifice leaving the 'dying sacrifice' as her last act of worship. The abomination would then be an outrageous use of the church by the beast, with an outrageous claim that peace had been made, and peace and safety for all would now follow. This might also be related to the wicked claim that Christ had already come.

Now back to the trumpet desolations. All of a sudden, three and a half years into the war between the church and the beast...No more Nice-Guy stuff! The composite picture is consistent with all three woe desolations. Number one is a description at the heart level of the impact of overwhelming numbers of demons and where the impervious strength of the saints will be easily seen. The spirits of evil will leave serious depression behind. The Spirit brings the full measure of the fruit of the Spirit: love, joy, peace, etc.[58] The mature child of God needs to be alert to the increase in demonic activity taking place at the present moment. One especially

---

[58] Ga. 5:22

raw expression of this activity is the popular Chinese discipline called 'Chi Gong'. When the author was visiting Beijing in the early 1990's, the government newspaper reported that 200,000 Chi Gong masters were in mental hospitals because of the deterioration of their minds. This Dark art is very attractive to many people because it promises power without moral demands. At that time in Beijing, I was given a video to watch made by Bill Moyer in which he extolled the powers of Chi Gong. The problem with exporting this movement is apparently a lack of demons to make it work. This will change when the Abyss is allowed to be opened. The first woe is then in the heart of the human race where depression (woe) reigns.

 *Sixth Trumpet*

Second woe - Robotic mass murder?

Revelation 9:12-21

> *The beast and the ten horns you saw will hate the prostitute. They will bring her to ruin and leave her naked; they will eat her flesh and burn her with fire. For God has put it into their hearts to accomplish his purpose by agreeing to hand over to the beast their royal authority, until God's words are fulfilled.*

This desolation, unlike the first five, is located within the symbolic categories of ancient Babylon. The Euphrates River, the lifeline of the ancient city, is the location of resident evil of appalling dimensions kept in divine restraint until a specific time arrives in God's timetable. It is almost like God was waiting for the river of technologic accomplishment which has become the lifeline of the Global Village to reach an inevitable level where life could be snuffed out by robotic machines. When this level of artificial intelligence that makes this possible is reached, it will be handed over to Evil so heinous that it could not be a player in previous human history. Elon Musk, the brilliant engineer scientist of Tesla car and SpaceX fame, went on record last year (2015) that the greatest danger facing the human race was artificial intelligence. He got more than a few amens, including Stephen Hawking of cosmology fame.

> *The first woe is past; two other woes are yet to come. The sixth angel sounded his trumpet, and I heard a voice coming from the four horns of the golden altar that is before God. It said to the sixth angel who had the trumpet, "Release the four angels who are bound at the great river Euphrates." And the four angels who had been kept ready for this very hour and day and month and year were released to kill a third of mankind. The number of the mounted troops was twice ten thousand times ten thousand. I heard their number. ... Nor did they repent of their murders, their magic arts, their sexual immorality, or their thefts.* (Re. 9:12-16; 9:19)

The first woe resulted in spiritual pain that drove people to seek death. The depression made them ineffective. They could see that the Christians were unaffected. The release of four diabolical angels and their armies was a different matter. One third of the world's population will be murdered. They are killed by fire, smoke and sulphur that came out of the horses' mouths. The whole picture seems like a scene out of a science fiction movie where robots do all the killing. The thousands of drones now in use by 40+ militaries and the research into military robots surely should cause us to pause in understanding how close we are to such realities. Again the sovereign choice of God is in play. "Release the four angels bound at the great river Euphrates who were <u>kept ready for this hour, day month year.</u>"[59] Three-D Printers are in process of development with the hope of mass-producing carbon fiber machines to replace steel as the material of choice. Once in production, 200 million robots will be a possibility for any number of nations. Note the divine restraints on the desolations:

- One third of the earth is burned up

- One third of the sea turns to blood

- One third of fresh water turned bitter.

- One third of light shut down.

- Abyss unlocked (previously kept demons down.)

    ✓ Could only sting those with mark of beast

    ✓ Could only last 5 months

    ✓ Could not kill

    ✓ Could not hurt God's sealed people

- Four angels chained were now released

    ✓ Could only kill 1/3 of mankind

- Finally Evil confronted and destroyed over time

---

[59] Re 9:14-15

As already mentioned there seems to be a connection here with the first fall of Babylon in Daniel's time. Then the Euphrates River was diverted, and the Persian armies walked unopposed into the Great city on the dry riverbed. If the West is Babylon, then the River meant is flowing in the West and the four angels chained under it symbolize latent Evil waiting to be mobilized. The thought is that the River Euphrates symbolizes the impressive technology we all glory in. It is actually to be turned into drones and robots programmed to do one thing: kill and destroy. It is also expressed by hacking into the banking systems, electrical grids, and military response systems.

Here is the core reality of Evil. It is so bent on destruction that it is as predictable as a wild animal. And when unbound will do what is expected. The angels have 200 million troops (robots) under their control. This woeful event seems to make no discernible change in the hearts of the human race. They continue to sin with abandon. They did not stop worshiping demons!! Is this a reference to Chi Gong? Apparently, the End will see an enormous interest in the occult, along with heinous demonic actions (mass murders and increase abuse of the weak and vulnerable). So what is this about? 2.33 billion people will be killed, per present population of earth. If this is symbolic of the desolation caused by the Anti-Christ, then surely this coincides with the destruction of Babylon described in Rev 17-18 and the end of the Global Village predicted in Isaiah 24 and the seventh vial in Rev 16:19. We must face up to this probable interpretation. The reigning, adulterous civilization which at present is the **Western global village of meaninglessness** is on the verge of complete desolation.

And, ironically, God plans to use the Anti-Christ/Beast and his ten cohort kings (Hegemons) to accomplish his judgement. Sooner than we think, the West will no longer watch lawlessness on cable news but will be instead watching their own cities burn and the world order melt away outside their very own homes.

Seventh Trumpet

Three-fold Intervention of Christ

Revelation 11:14-19

The timing of events is sped up by God. The great Angel raises his right hand to heaven. And he swears by him who lives for ever and ever, who created the heavens and all that is in them, the earth and all that is in it, and the sea and all that is in it and said "There will be no more delay! The great Angel announces that in the days when the seventh angel is about to sound his trumpet, the mystery of God will be accomplished just as he announced to his servants the prophets." The third woe is apparently multi-faceted, it will include 1. a strong church able to overcome evil as it encounters it; 2. the seven vials of God's wrath about to be poured out on the Dragon's Power structure and followers; 3. the smashing defeat of evil when Jesus returns with all of his saints at Armageddon:

> The seventh angel sounded his trumpet, ... And the twenty-four elders, who were seated on their thrones before God, fell on their faces and worshiped God, saying: "We give thanks to you,

Lord God Almighty, the One who is and who was, because you have taken your great power and have begun to reign. The nations were angry, and your wrath has come. The time has come for judging the dead, and for rewarding your servants the prophets and your people who revere your name, both great and small. (Re 11:15-18)

The amazing sacrifice, proclamation, resurrection and ascension of the church has moved the people of the earth to turn to Christ, before and up to his immediate subsequent sudden appearance in the heavens. All through the tribulation time of desolation, the church has been working to receive repentant sinners. Their presence on earth has been the difference in Christ's total victory over evil in terms of helping sinners escape destruction.

Jesus won the right to remove the seals that kept human civilization from succeeding. The result is the appearance of the reign of Christ within his people the church[60] just what we are reading in the Revelation at this moment: "The Kingdom of God is near; repent and believe the Good News."[61]

The third woe must happen in the days of this seventh trumpet which seems to point to the outpouring of God's power to remove evil from the earth to destroy the destroyers. In short, the third woe will be <u>completed</u> at the destruction of the forces of the Beast at the appearance of Jesus and His people coming with him in glory. But concomitant with the beast and his evil destructive ways the church will confront him and proclaim the Gospel successfully despite the opposition.

---

[60] Ep 1:22-23
[61] Mk 1:15

Revelation Light #*11*

THE CHURCH SPEAKS UP LOUD AND CLEAR

Revelation 10:1-11, 13:5-10, 14:1-13

*D*aniel says the battle is about truth. But who understands what is happening on earth at this moment? The last great civilization is on the verge of being destroyed by the Anti-Christ and his ten allies. But the church is proclaiming something both sweet and sour. And people are listening.

> *Then I saw another mighty angel coming down from heaven. He was clothed in a cloud, with a rainbow above his head; his face was like the sun, and his legs were like fiery pillars. He was holding a little scroll, which lay open in his hand. He planted his right foot on the sea and his left foot on the land, and he gave a*

loud shout like the roar of a lion. ... Then the angel I had seen standing on the sea and on the land raised his right hand to heaven. And he swore by him who lives for ever and ever, who created the heavens and all that is in them, the earth and all that is in it, and the sea and all that is in it, and said, "There will be no more delay! ... Then the voice that I had heard from heaven spoke to me once more: ,Go, take the scroll that lies open in the hand of the angel who is standing on the sea and on the land.' So I went to the angel and asked him to give me the little scroll. He said to me, 'Take it and eat it. It will turn your stomach sour, but 'in your mouth it will be as sweet honey.' I took the little scroll from the angel's hand and ate it. It tasted as sweet as honey in my mouth, but when I had eaten it, my stomach turned sour. Then I was told, 'You must prophesy again about many peoples, nations, languages and kings.' (Re 10:1-11)

THE CHURCH AS A TOWERING ANGEL

Revelation 10:1-11

This great Angel towers over Sea and Land. The scroll of the great angel is most likely the same as the scroll first seen in God's right hand. He has apparently eaten the scroll himself as he knows the sweet and sour of its message. In fact, this scroll from the hand of the One seated on the throne given up to the hand of the Lamb bearing the marks of slaughter is now in the hand of the angel whose stature is surely the result of his possessing it. Because it is indeed the Revelation that Jesus is giving us all. This Revelation makes the visible church a giant messenger who must be listened to. The End of the Age is sweet, but the details are going to be sour (fierce and difficult) to experience for the Church. "If we suffer with him, we shall also be glorified with Him."[62] And suffering is ahead for the Body of Christ. We who are indwelt by Jesus will complete the full tale of Christ's suffering for His church which is still in the process of being constructed.[63] "It will be a story about many peoples, nations, languages, and Kings." We are sent to disciple the nations. **This is a communication affair.** It is about raw power and authority to be displayed by God's people to those about to become God's people.

THE CHURCH AS OUTER COURT

Revelation 11:1-2

The church wearing the armor which is God himself stands holding a sign saying to the nations," Whosoever will may come." (in this context Paul asked for boldness)

> I was given a reed like a measuring rod and was told, "Go and measure the temple of God and the altar, with its worshipers. But exclude the outer court; do not measure it, because it has been given to the Gentiles. They will trample on the holy city for 42 months.

The Church Triumphant is almost complete as it waits in Heaven; but the final 42 months will be a time of great ingathering. 'Trample' has both a positive and a negative aspect. The remaining church will be on earth and, as the outer court, will be vulnerable to attack by the evil powers. But it will also be the instrument of harvest for a vast

---

[62] Ro 8
[63] Co 1:20-24

number of initially hostile peoples. This is exciting! In chapter 21-22 the church is 'The Holy City'. **These holy communities are the first stop on the way out of Babylon.** The church lingers in the suffering to snatch burning brands out of the serpent's clutches.

THE CHURCH:

2 WITNESSES, 2 TREES, 2 LAMP STANDS

TESTIFY BY WORDS, BY DYING,

BY LYING DEAD AND SILENT,

AND RISING BEFORE A WATCHING WORLD.

Rev 11:3-14

And I will appoint my two witnesses, and they will prophesy for 1,260 days, clothed in sackcloth." They are "the two olive trees" and the two lamp stands, and "they stand before the Lord of the earth." If anyone tries to harm them, fire comes from their mouths and devours their enemies. This is how anyone who wants to harm them must die. They have power to shut up the heavens so that it will not rain during the time they are prophesying; and they have power to turn the waters into blood and to strike the earth with every kind of plague as often as they want. Now when they have finished their testimony, the beast that comes up from the Abyss will attack them and overpower and kill them. Their bodies will lie in the public square of the great city —which is figuratively called Sodom and Egypt—where also their Lord was crucified. For three and a half days some from every people, tribe, language and nation will gaze on their bodies and refuse them burial. The inhabitants of the earth will gloat over them and will celebrate by sending each other gifts, because these two prophets had tormented those who live on the earth. But after the three and a half days the breath of life from God entered them, and they stood on their feet, and terror struck those who saw them. Then they heard a loud voice from heaven saying to them, "Come up here." And they went up to heaven in a cloud, while their enemies looked on. At that very hour there was a severe earthquake and a tenth of the city collapsed. Seven thousand people were killed in the earthquake, and the survivors were terrified and gave glory to the God of heaven.

THE SECOND WOE HAS PASSED; THE THIRD WOE IS COMING SOON.

Sweet: The two lamp stands that stand before the Lord of all the earth. Appointed as two martyrs, two olive trees, two lamp stands, angels held in Christ's right hand, Churches among whom Christ walks, olive trees sealed by the Holy Spirit to have the character of Christ and the Father. This in no way precludes the witnesses being two people as well as symbolizing the church communities militant.

Sour: clothed in the sackcloth of humility and prophesying for 1,260 days, a very turbulent and brief time. *The second woe is past* must mean that the conflict with the beast coincides with the destruction of Babylon and the attempt to destroy the Jews in Israel. The great preaching of the Church will call all nations including Jews to come to Christ. The Beast has set up his abomination in "Jerusalem" and the desolations are in progress.

Paul warns us that:

> While people are saying, 'peace and safety,' destruction will come on them suddenly, as labor pains on a pregnant woman and they will not escape. (1 Th 5:3)

The fall of Babylon, the death of the church and the return of Christ events occur in close sequence to each other!

Sweet: Empowered to breathe fire on those who would harm them and to devour them. Empowered to stop rain as long as they are prophesying. Enabled to turn water into blood. They can strike the earth with any kind of plague they want as often as they want.

Sour: And when they are finished testifying, the beast that comes up from the sea attacks, overpowers and kills them. Their bodies will lie in the square of the great city, figuratively called Sodom and Egypt where also their Lord was crucified. For three- and one-half days people from every tribe, language and nation will gaze on their bodies and refuse them burial. This indicates that the two are indeed the Church spread over the entire planet for all to see. The inhabitants of the earth will gloat over them and give each other gifts because these two prophets had tormented those who live on the earth. Is this striking down of God's people possibly the Abomination that presages the start of the earth's desolation? Brother Andrew said to me, as we walked together overlooking the ruined city of Beirut in 1991, "The church began with Christ on the Cross and will end with the Church on the Cross." Surely the sealing of the Godly Levy with the Father and Son's names through the Spirit will prepare them to die for Christ like the Apostle Peter in Nero's persecution.

Sweet: But after three-and-one-half days, the breath of life from God entered them and they stood on their feet and terror struck those who saw them. Then they heard a loud voice from heaven saying to them "Come up here." And they went up to heaven in a cloud, while their enemies looked on. Is this three and a half 24 hour days? Or is this another way to depict the last shortened three and a half years? As the desolations pile up, the church will become wreckage and her bones and flesh, and silence will be her last sermon in the darkness when no man can work. Their vindication will be to be visibly raised to life and caught up into Christ's presence. This will also be the spark that will fill the remaining people of the earth with faith to repent and call out to Jesus to be saved. The location in Jerusalem highlights the turning of Israel back to Christ.

Sour: At that very hour there was a severe earthquake and a tenth of the city collapsed. Seven thousand people were killed in the earthquake.

Sweet: And the survivors were terrified, and they gave glory to the God of heaven. (This is consistent with mass conversion which is related to what Jesus said in The Olivet Discourse when he talked about the elect being saved and about when he comes to where the vultures are gathering). The details will unfold as we go forward but see Rev 1:7 and make your own decision.

Revelation Light #*12*

GOD'S PEOPLE FACE TO FACE WITH ANTI-CHRIST

Revelation 13:1-18

*I*t must be noted that the war between Satan and the church began as soon as the church was born at the feast of Pentecost in 31 AD. Two thousand years of church history chronicles severe persecutions, shameless distortions of the Gospel, many, many divisive attacks using racism, nationalism, classism and ethnic strife, and from time to time massive killing of Christians...in the seventh and eighth centuries in North Africa, and...in the seventh to fifteenth centuries in Asia, East Africa and Syria at the hands of despotic Mongol emperors and Muslim armies.

In the 20th century, Christians have been slaughtered by Muslim armies and also by the Agents of Utopian ideologies that saw their greatest detractors to be real Christians, i.e. Nazi Germany, The Soviet Union, Maoist China. (In China, the Jesus Commune people were especially set apart for annihilation.) The apostle John warns his congregations that many Anti-Christs will appear from the very first century on until the end and they all will deny the incarnation of the eternal Son.[64] By this criteria it is clear that the message of Islam has always been Anti-Christ.

But near the End of this Age the final Beast will appear. All his predecessors except him have failed to take control of the entire world. The Devil controls much of the world but his agents, the proto-anti-Christs, have never been able to rule it all. One of the reasons for this is that people like Hitler, Stalin, Mao all seemed to eventually lose touch with reality, as the demonic evil in them couldn't keep from destroying them. And more importantly, God raised up nations to oppose them. This restraining work of God has allowed the church to carry out its mandate to disciple the nations right up to the present hour.

THE BEAST FROM THE SEA (THE ABYSS)

Revelation 13:1-10

> *The dragon stood on the shore of the sea. And I saw a beast coming out of the sea. It had ten horns and seven heads with ten crowns on its horns, and on each head a blasphemous name. The beast I saw resembled a leopard but had feet like those of a bear and a mouth like that of a lion. The dragon gave the beast his power and his throne and great authority. One of the heads of the*

---

[64] 1 Jn 3

beast seemed to have had a fatal wound, but the fatal wound had been healed. The whole world was filled with wonder and followed the beast. People worshiped the dragon because he had given authority to the beast, and they also worshiped the beast and asked, "Who is like the beast? Who can wage war against it?" The beast was given a mouth to utter proud words and blasphemies and to exercise its authority for forty- two months. It opened its mouth to blaspheme God, and to slander his name and his dwelling place and those who live in heaven. It was given power to wage war against God's holy people and to conquer them. And it was given authority over every tribe, people, language and nation. All inhabitants of the earth will worship the beast—all whose names have not been written in the Lamb's book of life, the Lamb who was slain from the creation of the world. Whoever has ears, let them hear. "If anyone is to go into captivity, into captivity they will go. If anyone is to be killed with the sword, with the sword they will be killed." This calls for patient endurance and faithfulness on the part of God's people.

The Beast has already been introduced as coming from the Abyss in chapter 10. This account in chapter 13 is a very compelling introduction of the Anti-Christ with allusions from Daniel. Chapter 17 will complete Revelation's teaching on this final agent of the Dragon. Paul has a somewhat similar description in 2 Thessalonians 2. And Jesus warns us first and foremost about the Devil's penchant to lie and deceive. "Lying is his language" said Jesus.

First! He comes up from the sea where he has been in some sort of storage mode. Peter tells us in Acts that at death

"Judas left and went to where he belongs." (specially assigned place).

Second! It had ten horns and seven heads with ten crowns on its horns and on each head a blasphemous name. This seems to be an incarnation of the Dragon with some differences in crown number and placement. It is important to note that the 7 heads together represent chaos and confusion. This is noted by psychiatrist Scott Peck to be the consistent mark of "evil people" he confronted in his practice.[65] It is impossible to get them in focus.

A guess would be that the dragon is a long lived being who has manifested himself in time through many empires while the Antichrist is one in a series of kings. With his imminent situation to consist of temporary control of ten Kingdoms. And through them he will rule the entire world for a short time.

Third! The beast resembled a leopard, had the feet of a bear and a lion's mouth. (reminiscent of the animal pictures in Daniel) He was given the dragon's power, throne and great authority. One of his heads had been fatally wounded but it had been healed. The whole world was filled with wonder and followed the beast who had been healed. They worshiped the dragon and the beast. What could this wound be related to in history? If this is a reference to the dismantling of the Turkish Caliphate after WWI, then the reference is to the revival of Islam as seen in the Middle East today. If this is a reference to the destruction of Islam in the Gog and Magog invasion of Israel described in Ezekiel, then

---

[65] *People of the Lie*, M. Scott Peck, 1983, Touchstone

it is imminent but not yet a reality. Along with the false prophet this seems to be a resurrection parody on the triune God.

Fourth! The beast had a proud blasphemous manner and was allowed to rule 42 months. It slandered God and heaven, waged war against the saints, and was allowed to conquer them.

Fifth! It was given the power to rule the world, so that all its inhabitants would worship him.

Sixth! God's people will have to be prepared for prison and execution. They must never stop trusting Christ. [note again the 42-month designation. This is happening at the very end and the time will be shortened by God. Just another reason no one can know the date of our Lord's return. But the important factor is that this time is short]. Later, this time of martyrdom will be repeated as a Beatitude, in Rev 14:13.

THE BEAST FROM THE EARTH

Revelation 13:11-18

> Then I saw another beast rising out of the earth. It had two horns like a lamb, and it spoke like a dragon. It exercises all the authority of the first beast in its presence and makes the earth and its inhabitants worship the first beast, whose mortal wound was healed. It performs great and miraculous signs, even making fire come down from heaven to earth in front of people, and by the

signs that it is allowed to work in the presence of the beast it deceived those who dwell on earth, telling them to make an image for the beast that was wounded by the sword and yet lived. And it was allowed to give breath to the image of the beast, so that the image of the beast might even speak and might cause those who would not worship the image of the beast to be slain. Also it causes all, both small and great, both rich and poor, both free and slave, to be marked on the right hand or the forehead, so that no one can buy or sell unless he has the mark, that is, the name of the beast or the number of its name. This calls for wisdom: let the one who has understanding calculate the number of the beast, for it is the number of a man, and his number is 666.

The drive to counterfeit the church is clear. This is not a new strategy for Satan, only its final version.

First! The third person in this unholy trinity is a lamb. He has two horns and comes out of the earth. Presumably this means he is in the stream of history. At this moment two major historic religions, both claiming descent from Abraham, are colliding again in a desperate culture war that seems to be driving Christians out of the Middle East. At the same time, the Islamic gains are coming at a high price as massive numbers of Muslims are leaving the faith. The second beast has two horns. Could he be uniting these wounded enemies under himself and the first beast in order to bring into existence a new combo religion, like "Chris-lam"? If successful, the prophet would be hailed as a great peacemaker. He performs miracles including bringing fire down from heaven. He makes the inhabitants of the earth worship the first beast who has had some sort of false pseudo resurrection experience. Wow! What an amazing accomplishment. Notice the false prophet brings about the abomination of the beast claiming to be God. Then the desolations begin.

Second! He deceives those who dwell on the earth, telling them to make an image. Now, if the image is formed by the followers of the beast then this image could be something like a political party or religious congregation. And it gave breath to the image so that it might speak and might cause those who do not worship the image of the beast to be slain. The two horns really sound like a fake Church / Mosque religious amalgam with demonic spiritual power to deceive the unwary and to kill their opponents. **All the utopian empires have been run by hard core party members.**

Third! A system of marks on the foreheads or right hands controlled who could buy and sell. This is done in the religious context of the false prophet. The mark seems to ape the sealing of the 144,000, Godly servants sealed with the name of the Father and the Son. In this case, they were marked with the name or the number of the beast 666. Its number is the number of imperfection, 666. What is being told us here? Wisdom apparently helps. The beast is after all only an imperfect man and his image is composed of imperfect people. He will not deliver on anything he promises. All the numbered will think like selfish superficial men and women. Most important these people will see the true Christians live and die for the truth with no regard for their own safety or attempt to save their possessions from loss. Not much different than what is happening to Christians, (Cross People) in Iraq, Syria and Libya today.

THE MESSAGE OF THE ANGELIC MARTYRS

Revelation 14:6-13

Then I saw another angel flying in midair, and he had the eternal gospel to proclaim to those who live on the earth —to every nation, tribe, language and people. He said in a loud voice, "Fear God and give him glory, because the hour of his judgment has come. Worship him who made the heavens, the earth, the sea and the springs of water."

A second angel followed and said, "Fallen! Fallen is Babylon the Great, which made all the nations drink the maddening wine of her adulteries."

A third angel followed them and said in a loud voice, "If anyone worships the beast and its image and receives its mark on their forehead or on their hand, they, too, will drink the wine of God's fury, which has been poured full strength into the cup of his wrath. They will be tormented with burning sulfur in the presence of the holy angels and of the Lamb. And the smoke of their torment will rise for ever and ever. There will be no rest day or night for those who worship the beast and its image, or for anyone who receives the mark of its name." This calls for patient endurance on the part of the people of God who keep his commands and remain faithful to Jesus.

Then I heard a voice from heaven say, "Write this: Blessed are the dead who die in the Lord from now on." "Yes," says the Spirit, "they will rest from their labor, for their deeds will follow them

All believers who find themselves alive in the world's last night must know these three messages by heart!

First! The angelic church has the eternal gospel to proclaim to those who live on the earth—to every nation, tribe, language and people. As they lived and as they died, they cried: "Fear God and give him glory, because the hour of his judgment has come. Worship him who made the heavens, the earth, the sea and the springs of water." The beast has been telling lies and denying the Creator and his righteousness. But the triumphant suffering of the church and its power to stand up to the beast was seen by all. And when they are seen to come to life and ascend to heaven everyone will hear the message and some with saving faith.

Second! The angelic church announced the Fall of the global village called Babylon. And when it happens the true intentions of the dragon will be clear because he brought it about as God had put it in his heart. In the end Evil cannot stop being what it is, Apollyon ... pure desolation.

Third! The angelic church spoke a word of doom to the followers of the beast. If anyone worships the beast and its image and receives its mark on their forehead or on their hand, they too will drink the wine of God's fury, which has been poured full strength into the cup of his wrath. Their message is pointed and terrifying ...they will be tormented with burning Sulphur in the presence of the holy angels and of the Lamb. And the smoke of their torment will rise for ever and ever. There will be no rest day or night for those who worship the beast and its image, or anyone who receives the mark of its name. The point is made that the church which preaches is also the church that must not surrender to the lies and schemes of evil. They must die for their message to hit home. A beatitude is given to underline the basic mission of the church. It is related to the original beatitudes of Jesus for it has been asked of many Christians down through the last 2000 years. "Blessed are the dead who die in the Lord from now on." "Yes", says the Spirit, "they will rest from their labor, for their deeds will follow them."

When five missionaries were murdered by Auca tribesmen in Ecuador in 1956, the women of the tribe were watching from a hiding place near the terrible scene of martyrdom. Jim Elliot and his four friends never fired their guns but offered up their lives instead. Twenty years later the tribal women confessed to Rachel Saint that they saw a chanting group of many 'flashlights' coming down out of the sky at the moment that the missionaries were martyred. Some of the men who had also been there spontaneously recalled the music they heard the group singing many years later when they heard it played on a recently made CD. (as told in a recent book written by Steve Saint)

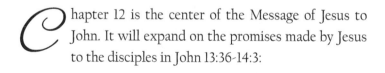

A PLACE IS PREPARED FOR
US IN HEAVEN

Revelation 12

C hapter 12 is the center of the Message of Jesus to
John. It will expand on the promises made by Jesus
to the disciples in John 13:36-14:3:

> *Simon Peter asked him, "Lord, where are you going?" Jesus*
> *replied, "Where I am going, you cannot follow now, but you will*
> *follow later." Peter asked, "Lord, why can't I follow you now? I*
> *will lay down my life for you." Then Jesus answered, "Will you*
> *really lay down your life for me? Very truly I tell you, before the*
> *rooster crows, you will disown me three times! "Do not let your*

hearts be troubled. You believe in God; believe also in me. My
Father's house has many rooms; if that were not so, would I have
told you that I am going there to prepare a place for you? And if I
go and prepare a place for you, I will come back and take you to
be with me that you also may be where I am.

The full picture is obvious in chapter 12. Up until the
time of the cross, Satan apparently was still able to announce
the sins of the human race in heaven before the throne of
God. Among other things, as a cherubim he may have helped
keep the people of God from returning to the Tree of life in
the garden of Eden, Paradise. The dragon's anxiety about the
child to be born harks back to the ancient Garden encounter
with the Lord when God told the Serpent that he would be
given a mortal blow by the seed of the woman. We see the
activity of Satan displayed in Job chapters 1 and 2, where
Satan announces his core lie that God's subjects are held in
check only by the perks God gives them; and if they lose the
perks, they will curse God. Job showed this to be untrue, but
he was not the perfect man. Until Jesus won our acquittal by
his sacrificial death, the righteous dead went to Abraham's
bosom, a place short of heaven. If they went to heaven, they
would have entered a barrage of accusations and
embarrassing charges from the evil one. For this reason,
Jesus said "Peter, you can't come with me yet"[66]:

A great sign appeared in heaven: a woman clothed with the sun,
with the moon under her feet and a crown of twelve stars on her
head. She was pregnant and cried out in pain as she was about to
give birth. Then another sign appeared in heaven: an enormous

---

[66] Jn 13:36

*red dragon with seven heads and ten horns and seven crowns on
its heads. Its tail swept a third of the stars out of the sky and flung
them to the earth. The dragon stood in front of the woman who
was about to give birth, so that it might devour her child the
moment he was born. She gave birth to a son, a male child, who
"will rule all the nations with an iron scepter." And her child was
snatched up to God and to his throne. The woman fled into the
wilderness to a place prepared for her by God, where she might be
taken care of for 1,260 days.* (Re 12:1-6)

The great sign sums up the absolute faithfulness of
God to end evil through the seed of the woman and to reveal
God's true glory to the entire cosmos. The incarnation will
undo the sin of Adam and Eve when the perfect man, Jesus
Christ, offers himself as the Godman for the sins of the
world. The apparent weakness of the man is not the whole
story as he is the coming King of Kings. He dispatches
Satan's lies about God and the cross, arriving in heaven with
our redemption won. As both God and man, Jesus ended all
satanic accusations, having become sin for us and then
makes us right by indwelling us through the Holy Spirit and
by resurrecting us to become the one new man in himself
whose home is now none other than heaven.[67] He has
prepared a place for us where he is also. He is in the bosom of
the Father which is our final destination in heaven. [Note the
use of 1260 days to denote the time period when the
'Woman' is cared for in the wilderness. This seems to point
to the preservation of Israel with an emphasis on her
continuing until the end of the time of the abomination and

---

[67] Ep 2:11-22

desolation at the very end.

> *Then war broke out in heaven. Michael and his angels fought against the dragon, and the dragon and his angels fought back. But he was not strong enough, and they lost their place in heaven. The great dragon was hurled down—that ancient serpent called the devil, or Satan, who leads the whole world astray. He was hurled to the earth, and his angels with him. Then I heard a loud voice in heaven say: "Now have come the salvation and the power and the kingdom of our God, and the authority of his Messiah. For the accuser of our brothers and sisters, who accuses them before our God day and night has been hurled down. They triumphed over him by the blood of the Lamb and by the word of their testimony; they did not love their lives so much as to shrink from death. Therefore rejoice, you heavens and you who dwell in them! But woe to the earth and the sea, because the devil has gone down to you! He is filled with fury, because he knows that his time is short.* (Re 12:7-12)

They triumphed over Satan by the blood of the lamb and by the word of their testimony; they did not love their lives so much as to shrink from death. Heaven has been cleared of Satan and his angels. We are not told how long the war lasted. We don't know how time correlates between heaven and earth. But we are told that Satan has been hurled down to earth. He is filled with fury, because he knows his time is short. This seems to indicate that Satan is focused on only one thing, the destruction of the human race!

> *When the dragon saw that he had been hurled to the earth, he pursued the woman who had given birth to the male child. The woman was given the two wings of a great eagle, so that she might fly to the place prepared for her in the wilderness, where she*

would be taken care of for a time, times and half a time, out of the
serpent's reach. Then from his mouth the serpent spewed water
*   like a river, to overtake the woman and sweep her away with*
the torrent. But the earth helped the woman by opening its mouth
and swallowing the river that the dragon had spewed out of his
mouth. Then the dragon was enraged at the woman and went off
to wage war against the rest of her offspring —those who keep
God's commands and hold fast their testimony about Jesus. (Re
12:13-17)

This section is a little more difficult to sort out. **First!**
The woman in the sign surely stands for Eve (the first
woman who sinned with Adam), and Mary (the mother of
Jesus) and Israel. After Satan was cast from heaven, two
great wars were fought between Rome and the Jews. The
Jews could have been annihilated, but instead they escaped
into the world of nations. **Second!** The mention of 1,260 days
and time, times and half time alludes to the last half week of
years of the 490 prophetic years laid out for Israel in Daniel
9. This short period of time coincides with the time of the
abomination when Antichrist is at his worst. In Luke's
version of the Olivet Discourse, Jesus speaks of the time of
the Gentiles being fulfilled. Zechariah describes 1. the
nations coming against Israel and Jerusalem to destroy them;
2. the supernatural return of Christ to bring reconciliation
between himself and Israel; and 3. the last-minute salvation
of the Jews. Somehow, Israel is preserved even in unbelief
until Jesus comes for them in the end. Jesus adapts the verses
on reconciliation from Zechariah to include the nations in
Revelation 1:7 NIV. **Third!** The evil dragon went off to make
war against the rest of her offspring—those who obey God's

commandments and hold to the testimony of Jesus. These are
the people of God: Jews and Gentiles who follow Jesus.

Revelation Light #*14*

THE LAST GREAT WAR BEGINS ON EARTH

Revelation 13,14

This vision supplies God's people with excellent 'intelligence' on the functional structure of evil relegated to earth after Christ's victory over evil at the cross. Prior to the offering of Jesus for the sins of the world, Satan seemed to be focused on slandering God and his image in mankind. Satan seemed to have broad access to the heavenly host to speak his lying message to them. The situation with man, on the face of it, seemed chaotic and unredeemable. The Accuser of the brethren was speaking partial truth about the sins of man and using it to call into question the future of God's plan to include Adam's race in the Kingdom. Up until the cross, God answered the Devil with strong prophetic words, including clear promises of a new Covenant; (cf Daniel 9). But the cross exposed all Satan's lies about God as untrue, by revealing the glorious reality of God's self-sacrificing love on behalf of man. It also revealed the full wisdom of God to remain the High and Holy One, and to remake repentant sinners into everlasting saints. The resulting redeemed community that emerged from this gracious act began to fill the earth with true stories of transformed lives. This multiplied the numbers saved and when the first wave died and went into glory **the next waves continued the work and died without fear as well.**

As Chapter 12 informs us, the cross authorized the placing of severe restrictions on the enemy of our souls. War against radical evil was prosecuted by the archangel Michael in heaven. When the dust settled, heaven had been cleansed from all evil and Satan was cast down to the speck of dust called earth with all of his angels. The Devil knew now that his doom was certain, and his days were numbered. Early on in this change of venue he tried to destroy the Jews. He failed even though Jerusalem was destroyed by Rome in 70 & 135 A.D. Many people died and the Jews who survived went into exile. The nations received them and frustrated the Roman attempt to destroy them all. And soon it was clear that God had suddenly changed his tactics and unleashed a redeemed and empowered church into the nations with the Good News of Redemption for all who believed.

The picture of a great red dragon (with seven heads, ten horns, and on his heads seven diadems) depicts the deployment of evil from the moment sin was found in him, down through this Age, and beyond.[68] In Scripture, the dragon emerges as a murky being, sowing into human thinking his deceptive lies. Adam and Eve, Job and his friends, the King of Sodom and his citizens, King Saul, and even King David had dealings with him. The Apostle Peter knew his influence well and called him a roaring lion seeking whom he can devour.[69] But as the dragon's pedigree is revealed, it is always partial and hard to completely define. He has no lasting place in God's plan for the ages. Indeed, the seven writhing heads reveal him to be the ancient chaos monster of pagan lore, a being hard to get in focus at best and difficult to defeat when he attacks. He lives to lie, said Jesus, for lying is his native language.[70] After the Deluge, the dragon has used ambitious people like Nimrod to forge empires to gain total control of earth. The heads are among other things symbolic of all the empires he has formed down to the present day. The prayerful pre-diluvian patriarchs gave way to the post-diluvian obedient Shemites who almost died out; then Abram finally left Ur to become God's homeless man (a Hebrew) and through him came several nations. The foremost of them was the Nation of God's people, Israel. No sooner had this community been formed than it became viciously opposed by the dragon. This has continued down to today and includes the international community of Christians. **It is no surprise for us to learn in Rev 13 that the last battles with evil will be between the last of the dragon's empire builders (the Beast from the Abyss) and**

---

[68] Ez 28
[69] 1 Pe 5:8
[70] Jn 8:42-44

a downsized but heavily anointed church (reduced from seven lamp stands to two). This holy levy will deliver its opposition to evil through prayer and solid proclamation of truth. Fire and plagues will fall from heaven on their behalf only until the angelic message has been clearly delivered to mankind. Then believers will become martyrs. And the earth will be filled with holy silence![71]

Chapter 17 of Revelation revisits both the dragon and the beast. It would seem that much of radical Evil is invisible to people in this Age. But since the fall, history shows that radical Evil has sought to rule earth, moving from empire to empire, and stopping often to confront and try to destroy God's people. Down through the corridors of history, radical Evil raises up his human agents and uses them to kill, steal and destroy. Jesus said, "all who came before me were thieves and robbers".[72]

This later chapter focuses on the punishment of the Great Whore and touches on the end of the final beast of Evil. Chapters 12 -13 deal with the war in heaven won by Michael in the wake of the war at the cross won by the Son of God. Then it deals with the war between the beast and the church which at first, like the cross, will appear as a defeat; but in the end of the END will be the cause of the greatest harvest of souls from the clutches of evil in the entire Age. In the conflict, the people of God prevail by proclaiming the cross of Christ, the word of their testimony and by not fearing to die.

The desperately angry dragon, knowing he is finished, throws all of his power into a last desperate attempt to wipe

---

[71] Jacque Elul, *The Apocalypse*
[72] Jn 10:8-10

all life from the face of the planet. According to Paul, he is under divine restraint until the very end when the restrainer is taken away.[73]

The nature of the restraint is seen when Islam, anti-Christian from its inception in the 7th century, tries again and again to wipe out Christianity and falls short again and again. From North Africa and Asia Minor, its advance into Christian Europe was summarily defeated. The ancient churches in the Middle East came to terms with their Islamic Overlords in such a way as to be allowed to continue but not evangelize. In Asia it was different. The Syrian Nestorian missionaries and their opponents the Greek Orthodox covered Asia with the Gospel. In the 14th Century, the number of Christians in Asia equaled the number in Europe.[74] Then in the 15th century, the Asian church was destroyed by Muslim and Mongol forces. The Japanese eliminated the Christian communities established by Francis Xavier in Japan as he carried the Gospel throughout Asia a century later. The Christian West conquered the new World and, between Spain, Portugal, France and England, made military commercial inroads into Asia. At one time during the Ottoman domination of the Mediterranean, one million European citizens were captured and held as slaves. Britain and France invaded Africa and the Middle East, and at the conclusion of WWI presided over the end of the Ottoman Empire and exercised considerable hegemony over the entire Middle East allowing a modicum of freedom to all the Christian communions present. The restraint of this most

---

[73] 2 Th 2
[74] Jenkins. *The Lost History of Christianity*

Anti-Christian religion has been consistent down to the present time. The restrainer humbled European powers one by one and all together in WWI. The Bolsheviks, the Nazis, the Maoists all failed to gain control of the world. Two superpowers emerged from WWII and neither gained world-wide control. But soon a final Anti-Christ figure will appear, complete with a religious entourage, a well-oiled political cadre and, when the restrainer steps back, will suddenly with ten relatively new power centers (hegemons, a state or group in ascendance over others) take complete control of the world. The goal of Beast is not a new utopian civilization but instead he will use his newly forged power to destroy the 'global village of meaninglessness'.[75] The main opposition to this evil will come from the church which will proclaim the truths of Revelation far and wide accompanied by plagues and fire. Then those believers will be defeated, and many will die. One third of the population of earth will die in this desolation. But the message of the Body of Christ will be seen as true, and many will call out to God and be saved. While the beast and his ten cohorts move on to mobilize the remaining world to resist the coming Christ, they will take time to celebrate the destruction of the Christians. Suddenly the bodies of the martyrs will be brought to life before a watching world and Christ will catch them up to himself where they will join all resurrected saints from the entire Age in Christ's presence. Shortly thereafter, the Beast and his forces will be destroyed by the brightness of Christ's coming. The destiny of the beast and all who follow him is summed up in 666. This is the number of man

---

[75] Is 24:10 *The ruined city lies desolate; the entrance to every house is barred.*

without God. All of them will fall short of their hopes and their dreams.

Revelation Light #15

THE LAST GREAT WAR ENDS IN HEAVEN AND WINE PRESS

The victorious 144,000, safe at home through martyrdom
Revelation 14:1-13

> *Then I looked, and behold, on Mount Zion stood the Lamb, and
> with him 144,000 who had his name and his Father's name
> written on their foreheads. And I heard a voice from heaven like
> the roar of many waters and like the sound of loud thunder. The
> voice I heard was like the sound of harpists playing on their
> harps, and they were singing a new song before the throne and
> before the four living creatures and before the elders. No one
> could learn that song except the 144,000 who had been redeemed
> from the earth. It is these who have not defiled themselves with
> women, for they are virgins. It is these who follow the Lamb
> wherever he goes. These have been <u>redeemed from mankind as</u>*

first fruits for God and the Lamb, and in their mouth no lie was found, for they are blameless.

Jesus gathered his disciples around him to explain the coming paradigm shift his death would usher in. The Temple, City and Nation would soon give way to Spirit filled people, Jews and Gentiles, who will form the Body of Christ congregations in a multinational Kingdom. This new model would in time cover the globe with the powerful personal presence of God. In the end, it would provide a people able to meaningfully stand against the powers of darkness come to annihilate Adam's race.

The warning about this coming persecution, as the birth pangs appear, underlines the serious calling of the church in the End. According to Rev. 12, the cross of Christ will arm the church with a threefold battle plan: proclaim the Death of Christ, testify about the changed life he brings, and display their ability to face death without fear.

When Jesus said he was going to prepare a place for us, he seems to be addressing the presence of the Devil in Heaven where he exercised his ability to detect sin in others and announce these sins in the presence of God and the heavenly host. Jesus Christ, by bearing our sins and the wrath they deserve, made the announcements of Satan 'old news' and the angelic armies of Heaven drove the fallen cherubim from God's presence. Heave became a safe place for the redeemed saints to dwell in forever. But the accuser landed on earth and there continues his vicious campaign. It is sad to see Christians square off against each other with satanic-like accusations that confuse and turn sinners away from Christ. The church is not called to accuse each other but to display through the Spirit the divine attributes of the

Father, Son and Spirit. Before the final end time conflicts begin, the church is prepared by the Spirit to think like the Son (in being determined to exist for others not themselves), to think like the Father (who spared not his own Son but offered him up for us all), and to think "come Spirit" and thus receive the fruit of love, joy, peace, patience, goodness, gentleness, faithfulness, kindness and self-control. **When the levy of such Christians is ready the final conflicts will begin.** The church will then proclaim:

- The truth about God (*the cross*)

- The truth about redemption (*our changed lives*)

- The truth about death (*our doorway to resurrection*).

The church will display God's people with the mind of Christ who will stand against evil, pray with cosmic power and convince the world to call on Jesus for salvation.

In the end, with the world becoming desolate through the work of the Anti-Christ and his ten cohorts, Christ will return early, and a massive harvest of souls will be taken to heaven by the angels. Then the wrath of God will fall on the forces of evil and put them in the winepress of the wrath of God Almighty. All who call on the name of the Lord will be saved. A video-like picture of this is found in the first chapter of Revelation where all the nations of the world will mourn at the appearing of Christ. Combine this with the throng noted in chapter 7 as beyond numbering from every nation who will be saved out of the great tribulation. God wins in the end in every way. (The maximum number in Greek is hundreds of millions; therefore, the crowd in Rev. 7 could exceed a billion).

THE LORD OF THE HARVEST GATHERS HIS SHEAVES

Revelation 14:1-20

> *Then I looked, and behold, a white cloud, and seated on the cloud one like a son of man, with a golden crown on his head, and a sharp sickle in his hand. And another angel came out of the temple, calling with a loud voice to him who sat on the cloud, "Put in your sickle, and reap, for the hour to reap has come, for the harvest of the earth is fully ripe." So he who sat on the cloud swung his sickle across the earth, and the earth was reaped.*

Is this the wrath of God at work or is this the promise of Christ as stated in Matthew 24 and Mark 13 concerning the great harvest of the elect saved by angels in the end?

> *Immediately after the tribulation of those days the sun will be darkened, and the moon will not give its light, and the stars will fall from heaven, and the powers of the heavens will be shaken. Then will appear in heaven the sign of the Son of Man, and then all the tribes of the earth will mourn, and they will see the Son of Man coming on the clouds of heaven with power and great glory. And he will send out his angels with a loud trumpet call, and they will gather his elect from the four winds, from one end of heaven to the other.* (Mt 24:30-31)

> *"But in those days, after that tribulation, the sun will be darkened, and the moon will not give its light, and the stars will be falling from heaven, and the powers in the heavens will be shaken. And then they will see the Son of Man coming in clouds with great power and glory. And then he will send out the angels and gather his elect from the four winds, from the ends of the earth to the ends of heaven."* (Mk 13:24-27)

Enough said. This is the final gathering of the saints as mentioned in 1 Thess. 4 and Rev. 7. The time has come for the time of tribulation to be shortened by the return of Christ, and God wins overwhelmingly. The description of stars falling, and powers being shaken harken back to the trumpets where the desolation is predicted at the Beast's hand.

THE HARVEST OF TARES TAKES PLACE

Revelation 14:17-20

> Then another angel came out of the temple in heaven, and he too had a sharp sickle. And another angel came out from the altar, the angel who has authority over the fire, and he called with a loud voice to the one who had the sharp sickle, "Put in your sickle and gather the clusters from the vine of the earth, for its grapes are ripe." So the angel swung his sickle across the earth and gathered the grape harvest of the earth and threw it into the great winepress of the wrath of God. And the winepress was trodden outside the city, and blood flowed from the winepress, as high as a horse's bridle, for 1,600 stadia.

That's a lot of blood! The wrath of God is just and apart from Christ, inescapable. This account unites the two dimensions of God's harvest in the End. One part is the final gathering of the elect from every corner of the universe, and part two is the pouring out of wrath on those who have been destroying earth in the Dragon's name; cf Bauckham.

> And the servants of the master of the house came and said to him, 'Master, did you not sow good seed in your field? How then does it have weeds?' He said to them, 'An enemy has done this. So the

servants said to him, 'Then do you want us to go and gather them?' But he said, 'No, lest in gathering the weeds you root up the wheat along with them. Let both grow together until the harvest, and at harvest time I will tell the reapers, 'Gather <u>the weeds first</u> *and bind them in bundles to be burned but gather the wheat into my barn.' (Mt 13:27-30)*

This is mentioned several times in the Synoptic Gospels (Matthew, Mark and Luke). The Lord of the harvest sends first **his disciples to invite** and then, in the end, **his angels to gather** his elect. Here we see the wisdom of waiting; earlier, some of the 'saved' were still trying to decide. The very End will be an intense few moments as some people will choose to stay with their possessions and family rather than join Christ. Note: At this point in the End, unbelievers have a clear choice to continue in hatred, or repent. No middle ground, and no chivalry/integrity that would motivate someone to honorably choose family over Christ. For this reason, using the word 'family' here, implying noble commitment to family, seems incongruous. However, there are other reasons to stick with 'family' in this context, as people must decide to put God first, or fifth, sixth, or not at all.

But concerning that day and hour no one knows, not even the angels of heaven, nor the Son, but the Father only. For as were the days of Noah, so will be the coming of the Son of Man. For as in those days before the flood they were eating and drinking, marrying and giving in marriage, until the day when Noah entered the ark, and they were unaware until the flood came and swept them all away, so will be the coming of the Son of Man. Then two men will be in the field; one will be taken and one left. Two women will be grinding at the mill; one will be taken and one left. Therefore, stay awake, for you do not know on what day your Lord is coming. But know this, that if the master of the house had known in what part of the night the thief was coming, he would have stayed awake and would not have let his house be broken into. Therefore you also must be ready, for the Son of Man is coming at an hour you do not expect."(Mt 24:36-44)

The "last second" aspect of this harvest will turn out to be glorious as many, many will choose Christ at his coming. Among them will be Jews and people from every nation on earth. The days before the gathering will be tumultuous, and destruction will be threatening everyone everywhere. Here and there a follower of Christ will be seen standing tall in faith and bowing low in intercessory prayer. All will be watching their every word and move.

For example, a recent testimony of an American pastor imprisoned in Iran tells about the constant encouragement given by the other prisoners during his 18 month stay. "We pray for your freedom" they would say when opportunity allowed. The church in the ebbing days of this Age will be smaller than now but purer and more powerful in word and prayer. They will be the overcomers of evil in the Night when evil reigns. They will die when they are done speaking and their absence will be felt and mourned by those who listened. Their deaths will be highlighted by the judgment falling on Babylon, the Global Village of Meaninglessness.

Revelation Light #*16*

THE FULL PICTURE OF THE WRATH OF GOD.

Revelation 15,16,17-18,19

After God's People are Out of Harm's Way

> *Then I saw another sign in heaven, great and amazing, seven angels with seven plagues, which are the last, for with them the wrath of God is finished. And I saw what appeared to be a sea of glass mingled with fire—and also those who had conquered the beast and its image and the number of its name, standing beside the sea of glass with harps of God in their hands. And they sang the song of Moses, the servant of God, and the song of the Lamb, saying, "Great and amazing are your deeds, O Lord God the Almighty! Just and true are your ways, O King of the nations! Who will not fear, O Lord, and glorify your name? For you alone*

are holy. All nations will come and worship you, for your righteous acts have been revealed.

After this I looked, and the sanctuary of the tent of witness in heaven was opened, and out of the sanctuary came the seven angels with the seven plagues, clothed in pure, bright linen, with golden sashes around their chests. And one of the four living creatures gave to the seven angels seven golden bowls full of the wrath of God who lives forever and ever, and the sanctuary filled with smoke from the glory of God and from his power, and no one could enter the sanctuary until the seven plagues of the seven angels were finished." (Re 15:1-8)

This seems like a repeat of the vision of the 144,000. But on close examination, it is the logical next vision. For here we have another view of the numberless multitude shown us in chapter 7. Here are all the redeemed brought safely out of reach of the wrath of God and the Lamb. They may have been in the vision of the 144,000 where harps are heard as background music. But here the victors over the lies of the Dragon are standing safe and sound. Fire is present in the sea of glass. This seems to be the interface between Holy God and Creation. What is now appearing at the edge of their place of safety is the wrath of God ready to pour out of the sea onto the earth. The people of God have escaped though through fire. And they are playing harps of God and the Song of Moses and the Song of the Lamb. This is a familiar situation if one remembers the exodus account where on one night the people were sure they would be slaughtered by Pharaoh and his army only in the morning to find themselves safe and sound in God's presence. Their joy is real and classic. The song is of Moses and now the Lamb has given it greater meaning as more people are saved by far than left Egypt so long ago. Indeed this multitude may actually include all the redeemed from every generation since Adam. They have exited the Age of the Knowledge of Good and Evil and they are in another Age with another time reference, the Last Day. Possibly we are there as well. The wrath will pour out of the ancient expanse (that separates the visible world from the invisible). This wrath will be poured out from 'I Am' the eternal triune God onto the armies of the Dragon on earth.

The multitude is worshiping God. And out of the Sanctuary of the tent of witness in heaven come seven angels with seven plagues. They were dressed in clean shining linen and wore golden sashes around their chests. One of the Living Creatures gave them seven golden bowls filled with the wrath of God who lives forever and ever. The sanctuary was filled with smoke from the glory of God and from his power, and no one could enter the sanctuary until the seven plagues of the seven angels were completed.

Questions abound in these Scripture passages. This might be the actual sanctuary that Moses saw when he met God. Then the Tabernacle built in the wilderness was an exact copy of what he saw. The interface between God and man in the tabernacle was a curtain. And only the high priest could go passed it once a year with a sacrifice. The Barrier between God and Creation is in heaven and it is symbolized by the wrath of God against all evil. During the Age of Decision, God held this wrath in check but now that the decisions have been made, he pours out his wrath on earth. The rest of these chapters in Revelation will chronicle this wrath in all its terror and justice.

Who are the angels? They could be Christians who are described in other chapters as being dressed in bright shining linen. This would explain what was said to John when he tried to worship the angel speaking to him. "I am a fellow servant with you and with your brothers and sisters who hold to the testimony of Jesus. Worship God for it is the Spirit of prophecy who bears testimony to Jesus." It is interesting that the multitude brought out of the great tribulation in chapter 7 is described as being:

> ...before the throne of God and serve him day and night in his temple and he who sits the throne will shelter them with his presence." (Re. 7:15)

The servants of the sanctuary would be priests and that is what Christ has died to make us. For surely the holy angels are angels, but Jesus taught that in heaven we will be like them and we will judge them. Is this outpouring of wrath a picture of our place as Christ's Body, near the throne of God with Jesus standing between Creation and God? If so then human saints have now been called to hold the golden bowls of God's wrath and are part of the answered prayers, they themselves prayed while still on earth under attack from the Beast.

The sanctuary is filled with God's power and glory which is what is in play at the end. Evil has tried to slander the glory of God and in the lying slander has caused great harm to people down through the ages.

THE WRATH OF GOD AS SEVEN VIALS IS POURED OUT

Revelation 16:1-21

> Then I heard a loud voice from the temple telling the seven angels, 'Go and pour out on the earth the seven bowls of the wrath of God.

 ## THE FIRST VIAL OF WRATH

> So the first angel went and poured out his bowl on the earth, and harmful and painful sores came upon the people who bore the mark of the beast and worshiped its image. (Re 16:2)

Remember how John was amazed at the beauty of Babylon the harlot. Now the first change is the superficial beauty is gone. Evil is surely ugly at its core, and now its lying seduction is exposed.

 ## THE SECOND VIAL OF WRATH

> The second angel poured out his bowl on the sea, and it turned into blood like that of a dead person, and every living thing in the sea died. (Re 16:3)

The world under the rule of evil was led to its death. Now God's wrath has no limits.

THE THIRD VIAL OF WRATH

"*The third angel poured out his bowl on the rivers and springs of water, and they became blood. Then I heard the angel in charge of the waters say: 'You are just in these judgments, O Holy One, you who are and who were; for they have shed the blood of your holy people and your prophets, and you have given them blood to drink as they deserve.' And I heard a voice from the altar respond: 'Yes, Lord God Almighty, true and just are your judgments.'*" (Re 16:4-7)

This leaves a kingdom of thirsty rebels with only bottled water and the specter of certain death all around them.

 ## THE FOURTH VIAL OF WRATH

The fourth angel poured out his bowl on the sun, and it was allowed to scorch people with fire. They were scorched by the fierce heat, and they cursed the name of God who had power over these plagues. They did not repent and give him glory. (Re 16:8-9)

Solar flares are a constant threat to life on earth and finally one arrives from God's hand, the *same hand* that has saved us from such extinction during the entire Age of decision. This is Climate change attributable to God alone.

 ## THE FIFTH VIAL OF WRATH

The fifth angel poured out his bowl on the throne of the beast, and its kingdom was plunged into darkness. People gnawed their tongues in anguish and cursed the God of heaven for their pain and sores. They did not repent of their deeds. (Re 16:10-11)

If this is literal, then the power grid is finished, and the darkness speaks of the complete loss of the technological marvels of the time and their reduction to complete humiliation and powerlessness. Jacques Ellul wrote often about the demonic dimension of technology and now the demons are without their screens, gadgets and instant, prayerless solutions.

 ## THE SIXTH VIAL OF WRATH

The sixth angel poured out his bowl on the great river Euphrates, and its water was dried up, to prepare the way for the kings from the east. And I saw, coming out of the mouth of the dragon and out of the mouth of the beast and out of the mouth of the false prophet, three unclean spirits like frogs. For they are demonic spirits, performing signs, who go abroad to the kings of the whole world, to assemble them for battle on the great day of God the Almighty. ("Behold, I am coming like a thief! Blessed is the one who stays awake, keeping his garments on, that he may not go about naked and be seen exposed!"). And they assembled them at the place that in Hebrew is called Armageddon. (Re 16:12-16)

This is the 'Post-Fall of Babylon story' writ large. In 530 BC the Persian army walked into the Great City on the dry riverbed of a diverted Euphrates river. In this time of wrath, the Western Global Village of Babylon will be defenseless and easy prey for a modern Persian consortium of nations to march West and destroy at pleasure. The victorious armies will coalesce north of Jerusalem in the valley of Jezreel, mysteriously called Armageddon, waiting for the arrival of the armies of Heaven on the great day of

God Almighty. This is most likely a *campaign*, not one quick battle. And remember, this is part of the wrath of God. **First,** the destruction of the last Babylon by the beast and his allies at God's inner direction; and **now** the destruction of the last forces of the beast.

 ## THE SEVENTH VIAL OF WRATH

The seventh vial of wrath poured out: Rev. 16:17-21

"*The seventh angel poured out his bowl into the air, and a loud voice came out of the temple, from the throne, saying, 'It is done!' And there were flashes of lightning, rumblings, peals of thunder, and a great earthquake such as there had never been since man was on the earth, so great was that earthquake. The great city was split into three parts, and the cities of the nation's fell, <u>and God remembered Babylon the great,</u> to make her drain the cup of the wine of the fury of his wrath. And every island fled away, and no mountains were to be found. And great hailstones, about one hundred pounds each, fell from heaven on people; and they cursed God for the plague of the hail, because the plague was so severe.*"

The details are clear and crisp. What is to happen to the last Evil Empire is proscribed by God, but as we see next in chapter 17 it is actually carried out by the Anti-Christ and the ten Kingdoms allied with him. World-wide hatred of the last civilization with its excessive luxuries will bring her down in a day.

Revelation Light #17

THE FALL OF BABYLON

Revelation 17, 18

The vials are poured not to bring repentance, but to bring judgment on the evil throng supporting the Dragon and his Beasts. The wrath encourages the organizing of the world to fight against the nation of Israel as described in Zechariah and other prophets.[76] The Lord plans to come to the rescue of Israel. The wrath includes first the destruction of the cities of the world, especially the last world civilization, Babylon. The actual destruction will come at the hands of the Beast and his powerful allies. The wrath overlaps with the winepress, blood that symbolizes an entire army dead, circled around Jerusalem for 150 miles outward, struck down by God's Son. It includes the destruction of 2.33 billion people by the angels unchained from beneath the Euphrates river.[77] Isaiah coordinates the fall of the global village of meaninglessness with the return of Christ:

> *One of the seven angels who had the seven bowls came and said to me, 'Come, I will show you the punishment of the great prostitute, who sits by many waters. With her the kings of the earth committed adultery, and the inhabitants of the earth were intoxicated with the wine of her adulteries. Then the angel carried me away in the Spirit into a wilderness. There I saw a woman sitting on a scarlet beast that was covered with blasphemous names and had seven heads and ten horns. The woman was dressed in purple and scarlet, and was glittering with gold, precious stones and pearls. She held a golden cup in her hand, filled with abominable things and the filth of her adulteries. The name written on her forehead was a mystery:*

BABYLON THE GREAT
THE MOTHER OF PROSTITUTES
AND OF THE ABOMINATIONS OF THE EARTH

> *I saw that the woman was drunk with the blood of God's holy people, the blood of those who bore testimony to Jesus. When I saw her, I was greatly astonished? Then the angel said to me: 'Why are you astonished? I will explain to you the mystery of the woman and of the beast she rides, which has the seven heads and ten horns. The beast, which you saw, once was, now is not, and yet will come up out of the Abyss and go to its destruction. The*

---

[77] Re 9:12-16

inhabitants of the earth whose names have not been written in the book of life from the creation of the world will be astonished when they see the beast, because it once was, now is not, and yet will come. This calls for a mind with wisdom. The seven heads are seven hills on which the woman sits. They are also seven kings. Five have fallen, one is, the other has not yet come; but when he does come, he must remain for only a little while. The beast who once was, and now is not, is an eighth king. He belongs to the seven and is going to his destruction. The ten horns you saw are ten kings who have not yet received a kingdom, but who for one hour will receive authority as kings along with the beast. They have one purpose and will give their power and authority to the beast. They will wage war against the Lamb, but the Lamb will triumph over them because he is Lord of lords and King of kings —and with him will be his called, chosen and faithful followers. '

Then the angel said to me, 'The waters you saw, where the prostitute sits, are peoples, multitudes, nations and languages. The beast and the ten horns you saw will hate the prostitute. They will bring her to ruin and leave her naked; they will eat her flesh and burn her with fire. For God has put it into their hearts to accomplish his purpose by agreeing to hand over to the beast their royal authority, until God's words are fulfilled. The woman you saw is the great city that rules over the kings of the earth.' "
(Re. 17:1-18)

The time of this vision should be correlated with other prophetic words concerning Babylon at the end of time. The destruction of earth is outlined in Isaiah 24 with two other topics, namely: 1. the return of Christ to establish the Kingdom of God; and 2. the imprisonment of the evil rulers pending final judgement. The destruction is simply the ruin of earth and includes the global village of meaninglessness.

The destruction of the last wicked civilization is described by Jesus in his Olivet Discourse (Matthew 24) where after the appearance of the abomination and its attending desolation he says that 'unless the time is shortened, no life would be left on earth'.

The first seal is introduced as a man riding forth to rule. He stands for all the human governments that vied for control of the world until the end. This stream of incompetent rulers is certainly one of the great limitations placed on our age by God.

The sixth trumpet warns of the unleashing of 200 million killers led by four evil angels who murder one third of the population of earth; (around 2.33 billion people). This certainly syncs with the warning that the Beast and his ten kings will destroy the harlot Babylon in the end because God will put it in their hearts.

The church of Philadelphia was told that the Lord would keep them from the hour of trial that is going to come on the whole world to test the inhabitants of the earth. This fits the trumpets and their accelerating intensity. The fall of Babylon will certainly test the inhabitants of the earth. *Especially* if it turns out to be 'Western Culture"

THE ACTUAL DEATH OF BABYLON

Revelation 18:1-24

After this I saw another angel coming down from heaven. He had great authority, and the earth was illuminated by his splendor. With a mighty voice he shouted: 'Fallen! Fallen is Babylon the Great! She has become a dwelling for demons and a haunt for every impure spirit, a haunt for every unclean bird, a haunt for every unclean and detestable animal. For all the nations have drunk the maddening wine of her adulteries. The kings of the earth committed adultery with her, and the merchants of the earth grew rich from her excessive luxuries.'

Then I heard another voice from heaven say: 'Come out of her, my people,' so that you will not share in her sins, so that you will not receive any of her plagues; for her sins are piled up to heaven, and God has remembered her crimes. Give back to her as she has given; pay her back double for what she has done. Pour her a double portion from her own cup. Give her as much torment and grief as the glory and luxury she gave herself. In her heart she boasts, 'I sit enthroned as queen. I am not a widow; I will never mourn.' Therefore in one day her plagues will overtake her: death, mourning and famine. She will be consumed by fire, for mighty is the Lord God who judges her.

When the kings of the earth who committed adultery with her and shared her luxury see the smoke of her burning, they will weep and mourn over her. Terrified at her torment, they will stand far off and cry: 'Woe! Woe to you, great city, you mighty city of Babylon! In one hour your doom has come!'

The merchants of the earth will weep and mourn over her because no one buys their cargoes anymore — cargoes of gold, silver, precious stones and pearls, fine linen, purple, silk and scarlet cloth, every sort of citron wood, and articles of every kind made of ivory, costly wood, bronze, iron and marble, cargoes of cinnamon and spice, of incense, myrrh and frankincense, of wine and olive oil, of fine flour and wheat, cattle and sheep, horses and carriages, _and human beings sold as slaves._ They will say, 'The fruit you longed for is gone from you. All your luxury and splendor have vanished, never to be recovered. ' The merchants who sold these things and gained their wealth from her will stand far off, terrified at her torment. They will weep and mourn and cry out: 'Woe! Woe to you, great city, dressed in fine linen, purple and scarlet, and glittering with gold, precious stones and pearls. In one hour such great wealth has been brought to ruin!'

Every sea captain, and all who travel by ship, the sailors, and all who earn their living from the sea, will stand far off. When they see the smoke of her burning, they will exclaim, 'Was there ever a city like this great city?' They will throw dust on their heads, and with weeping and mourning cry out: 'Woe! Woe to you, great city, where all who had ships on the sea became rich through her wealth! In one hour she has been brought to ruin! Rejoice over her, you heavens! Rejoice, you people of God! Rejoice, apostles and prophets! For God has judged her with the judgment she imposed on you.'

Then a mighty angel picked up a boulder the size of a large millstone and threw it into the sea and said: 'With such violence the great city of Babylon will be thrown down, never to be found again. The music of harpists and musicians, pipers and trumpeters, will never be heard in you again. No worker of any trade will ever be found in you again. The sound of a millstone will never be heard in you again. The light of a lamp will never shine in you again. The voice of bridegroom and bride will never be heard in you again. _Your merchants were the world's important people. By your magic spell all the nations were led astray. In her was found the blood of prophets and of God's holy_ *people, of all who have been slaughtered on the earth.' "*

The last civilization will be: awash in demons and extreme examples of excessive luxury, a source of temptation to adultery and all sorts of wickedness, a place of crime and sin, a source of unjustified hubris and selfishness, a materialistic city that majors in human trafficking, the killer of apostles and prophets, murderer of God's people and of all who have been slaughtered on earth.

This is not yet the description of America, but it will soon be true, and the entire world of cities connected to the West will become what has been described in the charge sheet of God. As the elite leadership minds let go of their grasp of truth, and instead make up stories as they go, there will benching to keep them from agreeing to support the growing antipathy toward God and his people.

The interesting aspect of the details of Babylon's sudden total destruction is that the desolation is carried out by the Beast and his ten cohorts.

Satan is Mighty

He is the "accuser of the brethren", and constantly tries hard to bring down God's wrath on us. At a future time of decision, many people will repent and come to Christ; then leave that evil City and be spared physical death. Satan himself will destroy the rest. This will be poetic justice for a people given over to self and sin; some will still deny that evil even exists. It is in the context of the increase of wickedness through Babylon that the love of most will grow cold. Also, this is the time when men's hearts will fail them for fear because of what is coming on the earth.

The Lord Jesus Christ is ALMIGHTY!

He promises that this Gospel of the Kingdom will be preached as a testimony to the nations and then the end will come. This preaching will be followed by martyrdom, the televised resurrection of the church, the end of Babylon, and the return of Christ with his own to destroy the armies of evil.

Revelation Light #18

THE MAJOR EVIL PLAYERS:

The Great Prostitute Rev. 17

 he angel who carries John away in the Spirit had been pouring God's wrath onto the Kingdom of Evil. He explains **the symbolic essence of the last and greatest civilization of fallen rebellious mankind. It is a woman living as a harlot** and using her charms to win the attention and friendship of the nations and their rulers. This civilization no longer has a goal other than selfish sensual pleasure, aided by the mind-and-heart-numbing escape of drugs to cover the injuries and destruction this brings to others. The world economy is based on this dynamic and hundreds of millions of petty leaders worldwide coalesce to form a unity with this debauched woman. She is dressed in purple and scarlet, and glitters with gold, precious stones and pearls. She holds a golden cup. But it is filled with abdominal things and the filth of her adulteries: (39 sexually transmitted diseases for a start; millions of abused children; millions of abortions; countless trafficked women; unremitting depression and cynicism, etc). She bears the name on her forehead: "mystery, Babylon the great, mother of prostitutes and of the abominations of the earth"; Rev. 17:5. Take note, she is drunk. Yes, drunk with the blood of God's holy people, the blood of those who bore testimony to Jesus. This is not a late activity. Babylon has lived as a Bolshevik, a Nazi, a Maoist in the last 100 years; and in the last 1,400 years as an Islamist has killed millions of Christians. But the Global village will vie with the recent past, in the number of Jesus' people killed. It will do so in drunken frenzy to stop the sobering speech and compelling lives of these followers of Jesus.

The Many Waters   Rev. 17: 1, 15-18

Ancient Babylon was surrounded by a maze of canals and waterways that facilitated the concentration of goods and peoples that served the life of the city. Water was the one necessary ingredient that, properly managed, allowed food and goods to arrive in the city and maintain the luxurious hedonistic lifestyle of the rulers of the empire. It would seem that the filthy influence of this civilization is not to be misconstrued as the actual radical evil powers themselves. It is to a great degree composed of 'unthinking yet grasping' little hearts who live without serious reflection. They serve an even broader group of people among the nations who were seduced into descending into meaningless existence where pleasure beckons but never delivers anything like life. It is not clear if these souls are beyond redemption yet. A strong case could be made that many will see the truth in a coming event that will wake them up to what is happening to them and show them a way out through repentance and prayer. These many waters will see God's holy people proclaim the Cross as God's essence. They will proclaim their personal experience of God in Christ as promised in God's word, and by **not** fearing death when inflicted on them by the Harlot and the Beast.

The Scarlet Three   Rev. 17:7-11

The Harlot, the Dragon and the Beast are all scarlet. They present striking images that speak of success, royal power and unlimited material wealth. The Angel chooses to bring John into the wilderness to reveal this wondrous civilization as it really is in a setting unsympathetic with pretentious evil. The true prophets all have a desert perspective in their ministry that frees them from getting caught in the dance of death they are exposing. The Woman is seated by many waters, but her power is derived from a scarlet beast. It is covered with blasphemous names, has seven heads and ten horns. Both the woman and the beast present us with a mystery, a mystery that initially seems to seduce God's servant and apostle John and causes great wonder in him. Possibly, he is shown 21st century skyscrapers in places like Dubai, airports with planes in flight, highways filled with cars and trucks, all accompanied by millions and millions of people. Or maybe the vision remains of a very voluptuous woman full of physical life and compelling demeanor. Either way the angel will have nothing to do with John's astonishment. John needs to see beyond the superficial into the reality of evil on earth down through the corridors of time.

Regarding "The beast, which you saw, once was, now is not, and yet will come up out of the Abyss and go to its destruction; Rev. 17:8...this being is a parody of the LORD, who is to come and rule forever. The inhabitants of the earth whose names have not been written in the book of life from the creation of the world will be astonished when they see the beast. The reason? Because he is a person of history who died and now has come back to life. Much will be made of this in the media and the angel exposes it as pseudo-prophecy. Only God can compile the list of the living at the beginning of the creation of the world. This wisdom comes to the minds of those who worship YHWH as 'I Am' and he exists in all of time and beyond, simultaneously.

The seven heads are seven hills on which the woman sits. The reference is to a final city like Rome which was situated on seven hills. If the details are illustrative, it must be that the composite nature of ancient Rome anticipates the composite nature of the final Global village.

> *They are also seven Kings or Kingdoms* (Note: same Greek word, basileus). *Five have fallen, one is, the other has not yet come; but when he does come he must remain for only a little while. The beast who once was, and now is not, is an eighth king. He belongs to the seven and is going to his destruction."*
> (Re. 17:10,11)

Here it is helpful to note that the symbolic name Babylon speaks for many historic empires of "similar ethos' that rose and fell through the years. Egypt, Assyria, Babylon, Persia, Greece, Rome, Islam compile a sequence of pagan empires that had dealings with Israel and Christians down through time. In this list Rome comes on the scene as number six (the 'one who is' during John's ministry). Islam as a caliphate doesn't replace Rome until 1453 and ends with the fall of the Ottoman Caliphate in 1920. This head actually dies as an empire. It was the short-lived number 7.

The beast is identified as number 8. This would work if the beast is more than a man. If the first seven are kingdoms, then the eighth must also be a kingdom ruled by the Anti-Christ. And one of these heads received a fatal blow! Could it be that the reemergence of the most avowedly anti-Christian empire, the empire that murdered three million Christians before it fell, turns out to be Islamic? At present three attempts to reestablish the Caliphate are in play: Shia Persia, Sunna ISIS, and Turkish Sunna. Of course other Islamic groups such as the Saudi Kingdom, the Egyptian Muslim Brotherhood, Al Qaeda, Boko Haram, al Shabab, etc. are vying to be heard as well. In the end, politics and religion seem to be taking center stage with strange alliances in the offing.

> "The ten horns you saw are ten kings who have not yet received a kingdom, but who for one hour will receive authority as kings along with the beast" (Re 17:12)

Note that both kings along with beast receive authority as kings for only one hour. The final run of darkness may indeed be very short.[78]

Note also the consistent assertion by the Angel concerning God's overall control of End events. The Lamb and his followers will triumph over the beast king's coalition at the Lamb's coming. In the meantime, God will put it in the hearts of the coalition to bring the prostitute to ruin, to leave her naked. They will eat her flesh and burn her with fire. To underline what is being predicted, we are reminded that 'the woman' we saw is the great city that rules over the kings of the earth.

This explanation raises several questions. Who is this woman? Is she the embodiment of the last civilization on earth? The present western civilization is composed of European and American nations widely influencing the rest of the nations and their major cities. The major cities of the globe are eerily similar in makeup and ethos, best described together as a global village. They are connected by secularization, capitalistic economies and socialistic governments. Christianity is fading as an explanation for the values and organizing truths of this vast village. Naturalism and materialism based mostly on scientism seem to dominate the accepted understanding of the meaning of life. Such meaning is very vague and strongly constrained by post-modern cynicism. The younger citizens are constrained more by their emotions and personal stories than by any of the transcendent religions. This leaves the door open for non-

---

[78] *Note: While writing this section, nine Christians were gunned down in Charleston, SC, by a psychopathic killer who sat through their Bible Study before killing them. Today, on international media, the surviving church members forgave the killer and implored him to seek Jesus and be saved. (6/20/2015)*

rational forces such as orgiastic behavior, drug seeking escapism, and a growing fascination with saturation of one's time and energy in entertainment. Here, sports and grand stories about the future predominate. This entire world-spanning culture is, therefore, at the mercy of radical evil and its lethal deceptions. It seems obvious that as the past organizing truths fade away, they will be replaced by religious exploitation and narcissistic political movements.

Note well that the present prophecy shows the nations of the earth linked to radical evil through the Babylonian whore. Is this connection stable? The answer is no. Radical evil has no concern for the advancement of civilization. The beast is reaching for control of the weapons systems scattered through the nations. Once in control, he will use them to a simple end: the desolation of all life on the planet.

Ten Evil Kings (Hegemons)   Rev. 17:12-18

The woman is seated on the beast but is not fully under his control until the ten kings yield their power to him. When empowered, the sitting woman becomes the clueless victim as the beast takes control of the world. At some point the beast makes the claim to being God and desolation follows. So, we have an influential global civilization that is suddenly expanded to become a global all-inclusive ruling empire, formed when ten new hegemonies coalesce around the recent appearance of the man of lawlessness and give him total power.

The Beast makes a covenant with the nations about Israel, along with a new Temple. Somewhere in this relationship the beast claims Jerusalem for his, divine worship and begins as rapidly as possible to destroy the entire world. One third of the population of the world will die in this sixth desolation.

Revelation Light #*19*

HEAVENS RESPONSE TO BABYLON'S FALL

Revelation 19:1-9

*After this I heard what sounded like the roar of a great multitude
in heaven shouting: 'Hallelujah! Salvation and glory and power
belong to our God, for true and just are his judgments. He has
condemned the great prostitute who corrupted the earth by her
adulteries. He has avenged on her the blood of his servants.' And
again they shouted: 'Hallelujah! The smoke from her goes up for
ever and ever.' The twenty- four elders and the four living
creatures fell down and worshiped God, who was seated on the
throne. And they cried: 'Amen, Hallelujah!' Then a voice came
from the throne, saying: 'Praise our God, all you his servants, you
who fear him, both great and small!' Then I heard what sounded
like a great multitude, like the roar of rushing waters and like
loud peals of thunder, shouting: 'Hallelujah! For our Lord God*

Almighty reigns. Let us rejoice and be glad and give him glory!
For the wedding of the Lamb has come, and his bride has made
herself ready. Fine linen, bright and clean, was given her to wear.'
(Fine linen stands for the righteous acts of God's holy people).

Then the angel said to me, 'Write this: Blessed are those who are
invited to the wedding supper of the Lamb!'" And he added, 'These
are the true words of God.' At this I fell at his feet to worship him.
But he said to me, 'Don't do that! I am a fellow servant with you
and with your brothers and sisters who hold to the testimony of
Jesus. Worship God! For it is the Spirit of prophecy who bears
testimony to Jesus.' " (Re 19:1-10)

The speakers list tells the full tale of Joy! A great
multitude, the 24 elders, a voice from the throne,
a great multitude, the angel. The messages give
the details of their joy! Salvation and glory and power belong
to God; true and just are his judgments; he has condemned
and avenged the whore who killed the saints; Amen,
Hallelujah! Praise our God all you his servants, you who fear
him both great and small: Hallelujah for our Lord God
Almighty reigns. Let us rejoice and be glad and give him
glory! For the wedding of the lamb has come and his bride
has made herself ready. Fine linen, bright and clean, was
given her to wear. Blessed are those who are invited to the
wedding supper of the Lamb. These are the true words of
God. What more can be said. This not a magical fairy waving
a wand. It is many, many people who have suffered much
expressing on the edge of eternity their joy for all to see and
join.

Early Intervention   Rev. 19:11-21

I saw heaven standing open and there before me was a white horse, whose rider is called Faithful and True. With justice he judges and wages war. His eyes are like blazing fire, and on his head are many crowns. He has a name written on him that no one knows but he himself. He is dressed in a robe dipped in blood, and his name is the Word of God. The armies of heaven were following him, riding on white horses and dressed in fine linen, white and clean. Coming out of his mouth is a sharp sword with which to strike down the nations. 'He will rule them with an iron scepter.' He treads the winepress of the fury of the wrath of God Almighty. On his robe and on his thigh, he has this name written: KING OF KINGS AND LORD OF LORDS.

And I saw an angel standing in the sun, who cried in a loud voice to all the birds flying in mid-air, 'Come, gather together for the great supper of God, so that you may eat the flesh of kings, generals, and the mighty, of horses and their riders, and the flesh of all people, free and slave, great and small.'

Then I saw the beast and the kings of the earth and their armies gathered together to wage war against the rider on the horse and his army. But the beast was captured, and with it the false prophet who had performed the signs on its behalf. With these signs he had deluded those who had received the mark of the beast and worshiped its image. The two of them were thrown alive into the fiery lake of burning sulfur. The rest were killed with the sword coming out of the mouth of the rider on the horse, and all the birds gorged themselves on their flesh. "

John saw heaven standing open. The Faithful and True

King is riding a white horse. With justice he judges and wages war. The armies of heaven were following him, riding on white horses and dressed in fine linen, white and clean. Coming out of his mouth is a sharp sword with which to strike down the nations. He treads the winepress of the fury of the wrath of God Almighty. The beast appears with his army and in the next scene he is captured along with the false prophet and thrown alive into the fiery lake of burning Sulphur. The rest were killed with the sword coming out of the mouth of the rider on the horse, and all the birds gorged themselves on their flesh.

The King stands looking into the Age of the Knowledge of Good and Evil. He is about to speak the Word that will defeat Evil in it and inaugurate his much-promised reign with an iron rod. **The overlapping of all events** is the key to coordinating them:

✓ Babylon's wickedness increases

✓ The Gospel of the Kingdom is completely preached

✓ The saints are defeated and martyred

✓ The lamp stands are raised to life and ascend to Christ

✓ The vials are poured out

✓ Babylon falls

✓ Christ is seen coming with his saints

✓ Many among the nations repent and are harvested

✓ The army of the beast is slain, and the two beasts
   are captured and cast into the lake of fiery sulfur.

   This is where the 'winepress of wrath' is trod by Christ, the birds
   are gorged and the blood covers 150 miles around the city.

Revelation Light #20

THE AGE ENDS IN VINDICATION OF THE CROSS

Revelation 20:1-10

God shows the rulers and authorities before him that a perfect environment could not have saved unregenerate mankind.

And I saw an angel coming down out of heaven, having the key to the Abyss and holding in his hand a great chain. He seized the dragon, that ancient serpent, who is the devil, or Satan, and bound him for a thousand years. He threw him into the Abyss, and locked and sealed it over him, to keep him from deceiving the nations anymore until the thousand years were ended. After that, he must be set free for a short time. (Re 20:1-3)

> On that day the Lord will punish the host of heaven, in heaven, and the kings of the earth, on the earth. They will be gathered together as prisoners in a pit. They will be shut up in a prison, and after many days they will be punished. Then the moon will be confounded and the sun ashamed, for the Lord of hosts reigns on Mount Zion and in Jerusalem, and his glory will be before his elders. " (Is 24:21-23)

The Apostle Paul tells us in his letter to the Church at Ephesus that God is teaching a class to the rulers and authorities of Heaven. One of the lessons apparently concerns the question: "Could God have saved the cosmos and sinful mankind apart from the cross, by simply supplying perfect government and sustaining a perfect environment?"

> His intent was that now, through the church, the manifold wisdom of God should be made known to the rulers and authorities in the heavenly realms, according to his eternal purpose that he accomplished in Christ Jesus our Lord." (Ep. 3:10-11)

God will take 1,000 years to demonstrate that the answer is a resounding NO!

Does God save only through the spotless Lamb who died at Calvary? YES!

GOD VINDICATES THE MARTYRS WHO LEFT EVERYTHING FOR CHRIST.

I saw thrones on which were seated those who had been given authority to judge. And I saw the souls of those who had been beheaded because of their testimony about Jesus and because of the word of God. They had not worshiped the beast or its image and had not received its mark on their foreheads or their hands. They came to life and reigned with Christ a thousand years. (The rest of the dead did not come to life until the thousand years were ended). This is the first resurrection. Blessed and holy are those who share in the first resurrection. The second death has no power over them, but they will be priests of God and of Christ and will reign with him for a thousand years. (Re 20:4-6)

A similar lesson will be shown by the recalcitrant evil prisoner who is Satan. He is a spiritual psychopath. And he will pick up his lying ways immediately on release and be cast into the Lake of Fire.

The martyrs rule the earth for 1,000 years and triumph. With Christ they rule with an iron rod. There are enough Scriptures in the Old Testament that describe this time which it turns out will be the absolute end of this Age. During this time, all will get a firsthand experience of how evil the unregenerate human heart can be. Only the cross and the indwelling Spirit of Christ can change this. The resurrection of martyrs into this fallen Age is special and unique. All the rest of the redeemed have been resurrected into eternity on the Last day. The rest of the dead will not rise until the Great White Throne judgment.

GOD SHOWS THAT SATAN IS NOT REDEEMABLE, EVER!

> *When the thousand years are over, Satan will be released from his prison and will go out to deceive the nations in the four corners of the earth—Gog and Magog—and to gather them for battle. In number they are like the sand on the seashore. They marched across the breadth of the earth and surrounded the camp of God's people, the city he loves. But fire came down from heaven and devoured them. And the devil, who deceived them, was thrown into the lake of burning, where the beast and the false prophet had been thrown. They will be tormented day and night for ever and ever."*(Re 20:7-10)

The Gog and Magog reference could be pointing to the revival of the Islamic heresy with its anti-Jewish flavor that nestles in with its anti-Christian core beliefs: God is not a Father and Jesus is not a Savior and man is not Sinful by birth. This bundle of lies will finally perish outside Jerusalem in a devouring fire storm.

Revelation Light #*21*

GODLY INTIMATE JUDGMENT

Revelation 20:11-15

The people of this age go one-on-one with God between the two creations of heaven and earth

Then I saw a great white throne and him who was seated on it. The earth and the heavens fled from his presence, and there was no place for them. And I saw the dead, great and small, standing before the throne, and books were opened. Another book was opened, which is the book of life. The dead were judged according to what they had done as recorded in the books. The sea gave up the dead that were in it, and death and Hades gave up the dead that were in them, and each person was judged according to what they had done. Then death and Hades were thrown into the lake of fire. The lake of fire is the second death. Anyone whose name was not found written in the book of life was thrown into the lake of fire. (Re 20:11-15)

The earth and the heavens disappear from God's presence and they are no more. In his book *More Than a Theory,* Hugh Ross discusses the possibility that the entire universe could be configured by God to be disposed of by God in a short time. The idea widely held view now is that the Higgs Boson exists in two energy states. If this particle is moved to the lower state, the energy released would cause a runaway fire-like release of energy that would reduce the entire universe to nothing in a very short time. This scenario is speculation but something like this is exactly what Peter writes about in his letter.

> *But the day of the Lord will come like a thief. The heavens will disappear with a roar; the elements will be destroyed by fire, and the earth and everything done in it will be laid bare."* (2 Pe 3:10)

But dead men are spiritual beings that are all resurrected before God as fully human after the thousand-year reign on earth by the martyrs. The saints are already resurrected and have been in God's presence since death or the coming of Christ. Apparently, all mankind must go one-on-one with God. Again this has already happened for the people of God who stood before the 'Bema' (judgment seat in Greek) of Christ after their arrival into Christ's presence at death.[79] At this moment outside of time, all will understand that the Age they left had its profoundest meaning in terms of what they decided about their Creator.

Paul told the gathered men of Mars Hill:

> *In the past, God overlooked such ignorance, but now he*

---

[79] 2 Co 5:1-10

commands all people everywhere to repent. For he has set a day when he will judge the world with justice by the man he has appointed. He has given proof of this to everyone by raising him from the dead." (Ac 17:30-31)

The people standing before the appointed judge, Jesus Christ, have all come through the Age of the knowledge of Good and Evil. They will be judged by what they did and decided when alive in this Age according to the light they had been given. They will arrive from the sea, death and hades. The question will be: Who among them is spiritually alive? Who among them has come to know by experience the Father and the Son? For, as Jesus prayed on the night before he was crucified "This is life eternal, to know You, the only true God and His son Jesus Christ whom You have sent"; John 17:3. The living have already been recorded in the Book of Life, the dead were judged by what they had done. If their names were not found in the Book of Life they were cast into the Lake of Fire. How does one get their name in the book of life?: by repentance and placing childlike faith in Jesus Christ as their savior from sin, guilt and God emptiness. In Old Testament terms, by calling on the Name of the LORD. Since the cross, they are immediately filled by the Spirit and come to life. To this salvation question Jesus adds, **"The first shall be last and the last first."**

Blessed is the one who does not walk in step with the wicked or stand in the way that sinners take, or sit in the company of mockers, but whose delight is in the law of the Lord, and who meditates on his law day and night. That person is like a tree planted by streams of water, which yields its fruit in season and whose leaf does not wither—whatever they do prospers. Not so the wicked! They are like chaff that the wind blows away. Therefore the wicked will not stand in the judgment, nor sinners in the assembly of the righteous. For the Lord watches over the way of the righteous, but the way of the wicked leads to destruction.

(Ps 1)

Revelation Light #22

THE ENDLESS DAY, THE ETERNITY OF AGES

Revelation 21 and 22

his study began with the development of a Christian Space-Time view of reality. It included God himself, this Present Age and Eternity. The case was made that the repentant terrorist who was crucified with Christ went with him to Paradise. Jesus, who is the resurrection, meets his own at death and brings them home to be with his Father and Spirit and Himself.[80]

These last two chapters of Revelation graphically locate us in eternity, symbolized as a Holy New Jerusalem, the bride of Christ. It is **a family portrait that highlights**

---

[80] Jn 14:16-23

the full restoration of Adam's sinful, fallen race that gives all the glory to God our Rock and our Redeemer.

> Then I saw 'a new heaven and a new earth,' for the first heaven and the first earth had passed away, and there was no longer any sea. I saw the Holy City, the new Jerusalem, coming down out of heaven from God, prepared as a bride beautifully dressed for her husband. And I heard a loud voice from the throne saying, 'Look! God's dwelling place is now among the people, and he will dwell with them. They will be his people, and God himself will be with them and be their God. 'He will wipe every tear from their eyes. There will be no more death or mourning or crying or pain, for the old order of things has passed away.

> He who was seated on the throne said, 'I am making everything new!' Then he said, 'Write this down, for these words are trustworthy and true.'

> He said to me: 'It is done. I am the Alpha and the Omega, the Beginning and the End. To the thirsty I will give water without cost from the spring of the water of life. Those who are victorious will inherit all this, and I will be their God and they will be my children. But the cowardly, the unbelieving, the vile, the murderers, the sexually immoral, those who practice magic arts, the idolaters and all liars —they will be consigned to the fiery lake of burning sulfur. This is the second death.'

> One of the seven angels who had the seven bowls full of the seven last plagues came and said to me, 'Come, I will show you the bride, the wife of the Lamb.' And he carried me away in the Spirit to a mountain great and high, and showed me the Holy City, Jerusalem, coming down out of heaven from God. It shone with the glory of God, and its brilliance was like that of a very precious jewel, like jasper, clear as crystal. It had a great, high

wall with twelve gates, and with twelve angels at the gates. On the gates were written the names of the twelve tribes of Israel. There were three gates on the east, three on the north, three on the south and three on the west. The wall of the city had twelve foundations, and on them were the names of the twelve apostles of the Lamb.

The angel who talked with me had a measuring rod of gold to measure the city, its gates and its walls. The city was laid out like a square, as long as it was wide. He measured the city with the rod and found it to be 12,000 stadia in length, and as wide and high as it is long. The angel measured the wall using human measurement, and it was 144 cubits thick. The wall was made of jasper, and the city of pure gold, as pure as glass. The foundations of the city walls were decorated with every kind of precious stone. The first foundation was jasper, the second sapphire, the third agate, the fourth emerald, the fifth onyx, the sixth ruby, the seventh chrysolite, the eighth beryl, the ninth topaz, the tenth turquoise, the eleventh jacinth, and the twelfth amethyst. The twelve gates were twelve pearls, each gate made of a single pearl. The great street of the city was of gold, as pure as transparent glass.

I did not see a temple in the city, because the Lord God Almighty and the Lamb are its temple. The city does not need the sun or the moon to shine on it, for the glory of God gives it light, and the Lamb is its lamp. The nations will walk by its light, and the kings of the earth will bring their splendor into it. On no day will its gates ever be shut, for there will be no night there. The glory and honor of the nations will be brought into it. Nothing impure will ever enter it, nor will anyone who does what is shameful or deceitful, but only those whose names are written in the Lamb's book of life.

Then the angel showed me the river of the water of life, as clear as crystal, flowing from the throne of God and of the Lamb down the middle of the great street of the city. On each side of the river stood the tree of life, bearing twelve crops of fruit, yielding its fruit every month. And the leaves of the tree are for the healing of the nations. No longer will there be any curse. The throne of God and of the Lamb will be in the city, and his servants will serve him. They will see his face, and his name will be on their foreheads. There will be no more night. They will not need the light of a lamp or the light of the sun, for the Lord God will give them light. And they will reign for ever and ever.
(Re 21:1-22:6)

This wondrous glimpse into the next Age is precious. Notice that the promise is that the apostle John would see the bride, the wife of the Lamb; then John is shown a marvelous city called the New Jerusalem. The reality of the people of God is represented by a carefully appointed city that functions in holy togetherness, unprecedented in this present Age. This carefully constructed unity allows them to become the dwelling place of God!

SOME OBSERVATIONS:

At a distance the whole city looked like a very precious jewel, like jasper, clear as crystal. This seems to place the city within God's holy limits as shone in the vision of the throne. Indeed this city has become the eternal resting place of the Creator.

✓ The twelve gates and high wall are attended by 12 angels. The wall is minuscule compared to the 1,500-mile cube that defines the city limits. It would seem that the entrance is symbolized by tiny gates and walls that conduct people from time into eternity. This scene is so phenomenal, so celestial. In the words of C.S. Lewis metaphorically describing heaven: "once inside the walls, newcomers proclaimed 'the farther in you go, the bigger it becomes!'"[81]

✓ The city has 12 foundations named after the 12 apostles of the Lamb. The symbols seem to emphasize that the city's eternal existence is based on Jesus Christ whom the Apostles represented to their dying world. Indeed the gates are manned by messengers most likely encouraging all who come to repent and enter by faith into the Kingdom of God. Every Christian who shares the Gospel is that angel at the gate.

✓ The Old Order passed away (tears, death, mourning, crying, pain, the seven seals are gone, Radical Evil is gone forever).

✓ For God's people and the people's God -relationship rules. Unimaginable unity reigns! No one this side of heaven has ever seen this except Jesus.

✓ God is making all things new ... i.e. new physics, for a

---

[81] C. S. Lewis, *The Last Battle*

start.

The wall was made of jasper. God's people are truly nestled safely in the heart of God.

The city was constructed of transparent golden glass. Like the Old Testament angels of the Lord, each person serves the glory of God in complete humility.   Self is finally freely denied yet serves.

The 12 foundations define a 'rainbow' which underlines the everlasting work of Jesus Christ in providing a salvation that will never end.

The 12 gates are 12 pearls, reminding all that finding the way to life eternal in God's presence is indeed the pearl of great price. The Age of Decision between God and evil is just for such discovery.

The great street, like the city as a whole, was made of transparent gold. Again the transparent person is the means of others coming close to God who alone can give us life.   As it is called to be in time now, the church in eternity will be a great highway to God Almighty.

The city has no 'designated room' for God. He is himself, along with the Lamb, the Temple The fact that the people of God are the body of Christ makes the whole city a holy Temple. In the words of Paul to the Ephesians The Church is the body of Christ, and as such receive the fullness of Him who himself receives the entire fullness of God.[82]

---

[82] Ep 1:22

Revelation Light #23

WHAT OBEDIENCE LOOKS LIKE

Revelation 22:6-21

I have made you light for the cosmos," said Jesus.[83] And that is what the city has become. It is full of the glory of God as he lives within them together forever. There is no more sun or moon. The big hint of hints is that the Church will be a beacon to other un-fallen peoples and rulers who will approach God by means of the city paved by sanctified humanity. They will see how to walk with God by watching God's people live with him in the city. And if any of these people ask if God can be trusted, we will simply tell them our story of living in the Age of Evil.

No more night. The gates will never be closed. They

---

[83] Mt 5:14

will forever see an endless parade of great kings bringing their splendor into the city.

HEAVEN AND EARTH WILL BE UNITED

The glory and honor of the nations will be able to walk from earth right into God's presence. Eternity will have a different makeup where a 1,500-mile cube of people will serve and pour life and light into who knows what kind of universe. Christ will truly fill the universe![84]

Caveat: Twenty years ago I had the privilege of teaching at a retreat with Dr. David Shenk, a highly published Christian apologist who dearly loves Muslims. As he opened the Book of Revelation to us, he stressed that the picture of the Church in eternity was the same as the Church in time. In short, all the truths embodied in the New Jerusalem—being a "city on a hill" for the world, or a lamp for the homes in the village, or a transparent highway that conducts sinners into God's presence from out of the nations or bearing healing fruit for the broken of the world—are imperatives for us all right now. The recipients of this teaching were Christian Somalis who went from the retreat into a nation that literally became a failed state, full of terror and destruction. At the retreat they read out the names of ten Somali Christian martyrs.

---

[84] Eph 4

WHAT JESUS EXPECTS OF US

✓ Keep the Words!

"Look, I am coming soon! Blessed is the one who keeps the words of the prophecy written in this scroll." (Re 22:7)

I believe this means memorize the Revelation given and keep it in mind...as each day unfolds, as a conversation topic when appropriate. Expect to experience blessing from the Lord as a continuing joy. One of the Old Testament meanings of blessing is: to be given insight about the way forward as things become dark and confusing; (Earl Palmer). Put another way...we will be led by our Shepherd because we have committed his words to memory all the way through to the End.

✓ Take ownership of your calling!

But he said to me, "Don't do that! I am a fellow servant with you and with your fellow prophets and with all who keep the words of this scroll." Rev. 22:9

Take ownership of your calling, given to all who keep the words in their hearts and minds. We are called to serve this Word like we were prophets of God or holy angels like Gabriel.

✓ Worship God!

I, John, am the one who heard and saw these things. And when I had heard and seen them, I fell down to worship at the feet of the angel who had been showing them to me. ... Worship God!" (Re. 22:8)

In Banias (Caesarea Philippi), Jesus told his disciples he was now on his way to Jerusalem where he would be put to death. He then invited his students to go with him and die. No one should entertain the idea that they can live for self as they follow Jesus, the selfless God. Worship of God starts with the denial of self and the joining of Jesus at the cross, where we die with him in order to find the resurrection life waiting for us. Life everlasting!

✓ Understand time from God's perspective.

"Look, I am coming soon!

The angel said to me, "These words are trustworthy and true. The Lord, the God who inspires the prophets, sent his angel to show his servants the things that must soon take place." Then he told me, "Do not seal up the words of the prophecy of this scroll, because the time is near. Let the one who does wrong continue to do wrong; let the vile person continue to be vile; let the one who does right continue to do right; and let the holy person continue to be holy." (Re 22:6,1-11)

"Look, I am coming soon! My reward is with me, and I will give to each person according to what they have done. I am the Alpha and the Omega, the First and the Last, the Beginning and the End.

(Re 22:12-14)

He who testifies to these things says, "Yes, I am coming soon."
(Re 22:20)

We discussed this at the beginning of the prophetic truths and again at the beginning of this Book of Revelation. If the Last Day, mentioned in Genesis 2 and John 5 and 6 and 11, is the time of our death[85] at the edge of eternity, and we are transported in resurrection power into Christ's presence, then every one of us is less than one lifetime from eternity and the fulfillment of the Revelation. Memorize this word and think about it hour by hour. We will never die! Dallas Willard was quoted by his pastor as saying that 'he would not be surprised if he didn't realize he was dead until several weeks into heaven'. As the End becomes very dark, we are still waiting for Jesus to come for us...not death!

✓ Our hope Is Jesus' blood and righteousness.

Blessed are those who wash their robes, that they may have the right to the tree of life and may go through the gates into the city. Outside are the dogs, those who practice magic arts, the sexually immoral, the murderers, the idolaters and everyone who loves and practices falsehood. 22:14-15

The most ancient way of understanding salvation comes from Genesis 2 & 3 where stands the Tree of Life and a way back into Eden guarded by cherubim. We are dogs,

---

[85] 2 Co 5:1

gripped by magic and superstition, immoral to the core, murderers, idol worshipers and liars, until plunged by grace through faith into the cleansing flood of Immanuel's blood and transformed by the Spirit's new birthing power.

✓ This Word of truth is a community word.

> "I, Jesus, have sent my angel to give you this testimony for the churches. I am the Root and the Offspring of David, and the bright Morning Star." (Re 22:16)

Everyone in each church should live out their relationships in the light of what is coming. We are on the edge of **perfect Christian oneness** that is so beyond what we have ever experienced; it is on a par with Christ overcoming John with his full transcendent glory! And when we see him, we shall be like him.

✓ Say it and mean it: "I am thirsty for God.

> The Spirit and the bride say, "Come!" And let the one who hears say, "Come!" Let the one who is thirsty come; and let the one who wishes take the free gift of the water of life. (Re 22:17)

I want all there is of Him to be my life for eternity." Or in the words of converted Christian-killer Paul, "Let the Holy Spirit go on filling you!"[86] Now!

---

[86] Ep 5:18

✓ Don't try to change the text of this Word.

I warn everyone who hears the words of the prophecy of this scroll: If anyone adds anything to them, God will add to that person the plagues described in this scroll. And if anyone takes words away from this scroll of prophecy, God will take away from that person any share in the tree of life and in the Holy City, which are described in this scroll.

Amen. Come, Lord Jesus.

The grace of the Lord Jesus be with God's people. Amen.
(Re 22:18-21)

It is the living Word of the living God. We live in the Age of the knowledge of Good and the knowledge of Evil. Instead, say **Amen** to it and it will change you. Then say, Come Lord Jesus, and make me just like You.[87]

---

[87] 1 Jn 3

Postscript

*T*he city is an enormous perfect cube, just like the Holy of Holies in the tabernacle built by Moses. The gates of the city are never shut as the two rooms of the past Age have been replaced by one room. The invitation is spectacular: **"Whosoever will may came and drink and live!"**[88] All believers in this Age are one heartbeat from taking their place in this city of God in eternity. The promise made to Abraham by God, "I am your shield and your very great reward," is for us as well.

Ending this present Age is a huge undertaking by God. The elimination of Evil has been a foregone conclusion since the birth of Jesus.

It's time to take a deep breath and stand back and reflect for a moment. Many of the popular theologies of the End seem to downplay the calling of the church to be stars

---

[88] Re 22:17

and angels in Christ's right hand. Some insist that the church
in Christ's right hand will be removed before the tribulation
starts and will not be called on to do anything. Isaiah, Daniel
and Jesus seem to say just the opposite, and Paul seems to
echo their prophetic words in Ephesians 6, Romans 8,
Colossians 1, and 2 Corinthians 5.

Often Christian communions compete, slander or just
ignore each other, not realizing how this plays into the hope
of radical evil to disempower the church. Our corporate
credibility requires that we love each other as Christ loves
us.

The Global village civilization with its all-consuming
technology seriously limits the church in prayer, and the
switches of the same technology seem to preclude the need
for faith to do anything. And into the prayerlessness comes
mind and soul-numbing wickedness and lies that
categorically keep this generation from even seeking the
truth.

Freedom, choice, materialism, and poor education
provide doorways to self-aggrandizement. The steady attack
of Marxism and its antithesis, post modernism, have set the
agenda for most campuses, alienating the older generation
that has learned by hard experience that truth matters, and
utopian ideas are just that: pipe dreams. But, of course, **God
is in control.** So, parents and friends must be willing to
redemptively assuage the loneliness and unhappiness
produced by lack of meaning in their loved ones' lives.

And, last of all, as we keep the words of Revelation in
our memories and conscious minds, we see that vast throng
beyond numbering that God promises will come to Christ in
the end, through the stark realities of the tribulation.

God wins!

Bibliography

A Greek-English Lexicon of the New Testament and Other Early Christian Literature, Bauer,1979, U. of Chicago.

Apocalypse, J. Ellul,1977, The Seabury Press

Daniel, J. Baldwin,1978, IVP TOTC

Escape from Reason, F. Schaeffer,1968, IVP

Exploring Revelation, J. B. Phillips,1974, Moody

Finding God in Ancient China, Chan Kei Thong,2009, Zondervan

Improbable Planet, H. Ross,2016, 2016.. Baker.

Isaiah By the Day, A. Moyter,2011, Christian Focus

Lost History of Christianity, J. P. Jenkins,2008, HarperOne.

Mere Christianity, C. S. Lewis, 1952, HarperCollins

Navigating Genesis, H. Ross,2014, RTB Press

One, Two, Three...Infinity, G. Gammow,1947, Gamow

Phaedo, Plato

Philosophy and the Christian Faith, C. Brown,1969, InterVarsity

Revelation of John, George Eldon Ladd,1972, Eerdmans

Revelation, Ramsey Michaels,1997, IVPNTCS

Revelation, L. Morris,1987, IVP

The Book of Revelation, R. H. Mounce,1977, Eerdmans

The Chronicles of Narnia, C. S. Lewis, 1950-56, HarperCollins

The Climax of Prophecy, R. Bauckham,1993, T&T Clark

The Creator and the Cosmos, Hugh Ross,2001, Reason to Believe

The Fingerprint of God, Hugh Ross, 1989, Whitaker House

The Gathering Storm, T. J. Daley, 1992, Chosen Books

The Gospel According to John, D. A. Carson, 1991, IVP

The Meaning of Persons, P. Tournier, 1957, Harper and Row

People of the Lie, M. Scott Peck, 1983, Touchstone

The Problem of Pain, C. S. Lewis, 1940, HarperOne

The Prophecy of Isaiah, A. Moyter, 1993, IVP

The Saving Life of Christ, M. I. Thomas, Zondervan, 1988

The Space Trilogy, C. S. Lewis, 1938-45, The Bodley Head

The Theology of the Book of Revelation, R. Bauckham, 1993, Cambridge

INDEX OF BIBLICAL PASSAGES

Old Testament

New Testament